HOW AMERICA COOKS TODAY

Woman's Day®
CHICKEN
AND POULTRY

Sedgewood® Press

New York

Photographer Credits

Ben Calvo: pages 11 (top), 14, 16, 17, 36, 37, 39, 43, 50, 51, 63, 64, 78, 106, 119, 126

Jim Coit: page 111

John P. Endress: page 112

Katrina Filary: pages 20, 22, 24, 26, 27, 56

Michael Skopt: page 73

Eleanor Thompson: page 69

Marcus Tullis: page 72

Tim Turner: pages 70, 74, 85

John Uher: pages 4, 7, 8, 11 (bottom), 12, 15, 28, 32, 34, 40, 42, 44, 46, 48, 52, 59, 60, 62, 76, 81, 89, 90, 92, 93, 94, 95, 97, 98, 104, 107, 108, 110, 114, 115, 116, 120, 122, 124

Please address your correspondence to
Customer Service Department,
Sedgewood® Press, Meredith Corporation,
150 East 52nd Street, New York, NY 10022.

For DIAMANDIS COMMUNICATIONS INC.

Editor-in-Chief, *Woman's Day:* Ellen R. Levine
Food Editor: Elizabeth Alston
Researchers: Mary Rieger, Marinella Cancio

For SEDGEWOOD® PRESS

Director: Elizabeth P. Rice
Editorial Director: Alison Brown Cerier
Project Editor: Miriam Rubin
Copy Editor: Joan Michel
Production Manager: Bill Rose
Designer: Remo Cosentino

Contents

RECIPE SYMBOLS

At the beginning of many recipes are symbols pointing out which dishes are:

♥ **LOW-CALORIE** (main-dish serving under 300 calories)

◔ **MAKE-AHEAD** (part or all of the recipe can or should be made ahead)

✳ **MICROWAVE** (recipe or variation)

★ **SPECIAL—AND WORTH IT** (in terms of time, calories or expense)

In the Skillet

Skillet cooking is your shortcut to the dinner table. Pan-fry chicken or turkey cutlets in just minutes, then make a succulent sauce right in the skillet— or make a complete hearty meal in one skillet.

Dilled Chicken Fricassee with
New Potatoes and Green Beans

Hearty Skillet Meals

Cleanup time can be over in almost no time if you make a whole main course, including vegetables, in one pan.

Dilled Chicken Fricassee with New Potatoes and Green Beans

Dill is often sold in a large bunch, so you'll have plenty left over for adding zip to other dishes. Add fresh dill to a cucumber and bell-pepper salad, sprinkle it over broiled fish or stir it into sour cream for a baked-potato topping.

⅓ cup all-purpose flour
1 teaspoon salt
½ teaspoon paprika
4 chicken-breast halves (about 8 ounces each)
2 tablespoons vegetable oil
2 cups chicken broth
¼ cup snipped fresh dill
8 small thin-skinned new potatoes (about 12 ounces)
12 ounces fresh green beans, trimmed
1 tablespoon lemon juice, or to taste

1. Mix flour, salt and paprika on a sheet of waxed paper. Coat chicken in flour mixture, reserving leftover flour.

2. Heat oil in a large, high-sided skillet over high heat. Add chicken skin-side down and brown 3 minutes. Turn chicken.

3. Stir reserved flour mixture into skillet. Gradually stir in chicken broth, then 2 tablespoons of the dill, and bring to a boil.

4. Add potatoes. Reduce heat to low. Cover and simmer 10 minutes.

5. Add green beans. Cover and simmer 10 minutes longer, until chicken and potatoes are fork-tender and beans are crisp-tender.

6. Stir in lemon juice and sprinkle with remaining dill. Transfer to a heated platter and serve.

Makes 4 servings. Per serving: 475 calories, 52 grams protein, 28 grams carbohydrate, 16 grams fat, 121 milligrams cholesterol, 999 milligrams sodium

Skillet Chicken Breasts Parmigiana with Yellow Summer Squash and Green Beans

Serve with hot rolls or a good bread and fresh fruit for dessert. If you prefer, use zucchini instead of yellow summer squash.

2 tablespoons vegetable oil
3 large cloves garlic, halved
4 boned and skinned chicken-breast halves (about 5 ounces each)
¾ teaspoon salt
½ teaspoon pepper
2 medium-size yellow summer squash (about 12 ounces), thinly sliced
1½ cups cooked fresh or thawed frozen cut green beans
½ teaspoon dried oregano leaves
4 slices (1 ounce each) mozzarella cheese
⅔ cup prepared spaghetti sauce

1. Heat oil in a large heavy skillet over medium heat. Add garlic and cook until golden. Lift garlic from oil with a slotted spoon and discard.

2. Add chicken to skillet and cook about 3 minutes per side, until no longer pink in the center. Season with ¼ teaspoon of the salt and ⅛ teaspoon of the pepper. Remove from the skillet to a plate.

3. Add squash and green beans to skillet. Sprinkle with oregano and remaining salt and pepper. Cook about 5 minutes, stirring occasionally, until squash is crisp-tender and beans are hot. Push to sides of skillet.

4. Arrange chicken in center of skillet. Top each breast half with a slice of cheese, then spoon on sauce. Cover and cook 5 to 7 minutes, until cheese melts and sauce is hot. Transfer to a heated platter and serve.

Makes 4 servings. Per serving: 439 calories, 53 grams protein, 13 grams carbohydrate, 19 grams fat, 134 milligrams cholesterol, 854 milligrams sodium

Breast of Chicken Rustica

Breast of Chicken Rustica

The noodles cook to perfection right in the skillet along with the other ingredients. Serve with a loaf of crusty bread and, for dessert, crisp apples or orange wedges. You can reduce the calories in this recipe by using skim or low-fat milk.

2 tablespoons butter or margarine
4 boned and skinned chicken-breast
   halves (about 5 ounces each)
1½ cups boiling water
1½ cups milk
1 package (2.7 ounces) Swiss tomato-
   with-basil soup mix
5 ounces (3 cups) medium
   egg noodles
1 can (8½ ounces) artichoke hearts,
   drained and halved
1 package (10 ounces) frozen whole
   green beans
1 can (4 ounces) button mushrooms,
   drained

1. Melt butter in a large skillet over high heat. Add chicken-breast halves skinned-side down. Brown about 3 minutes, until golden. Turn chicken.

2. Add water, milk and soup mix to skillet. Stir to blend. Sprinkle noodles over top and stir to cover with liquid.

3. Add artichoke hearts, green beans and mushrooms to skillet.

4. Cover and bring to a boil. Reduce heat to medium-low and simmer 7 to 9 minutes, stirring twice, until chicken is no longer pink in the center and noodles are tender. Transfer to a heated platter and serve.

Makes 4 servings. Per serving: 661 calories, 59 grams protein, 52 grams carbohydrate, 23 grams fat, 178 milligrams cholesterol with butter, 160 milligrams cholesterol with margarine, 1,000 milligrams sodium

Chicken Breasts with Arugula Salsa, Broccoli and Cauliflower

Arugula (also called rocket), a peppery green, is a member of the mustard family. Watercress would be a very good substitute.

1 large ripe fresh tomato (about 8 ounces), coarsely chopped
3 ounces arugula (about 1½ cups loosely packed), tough stems trimmed, rinsed and coarsely chopped (about 1¼ cups chopped)
4 tablespoons olive oil
1 tablespoon red-wine vinegar
¼ teaspoon pepper
1 large egg
½ cup packaged Italian-style dry bread crumbs
4 boned and skinned chicken-breast halves (about 4 ounces each)
1 cup water
1 package (10 ounces) frozen cauliflower
1 package (10 ounces) frozen broccoli
2 tablespoons butter or margarine
1 teaspoon dried basil leaves
¼ teaspoon salt

1. To make salsa: Mix tomato, arugula, 2 tablespoons of the oil, the vinegar and pepper in a medium-size bowl.

2. To make chicken: Beat egg in a pie plate. Spread crumbs on a sheet of waxed paper. Dip chicken in egg, then coat in crumbs.

3. Heat remaining 2 tablespoons oil in a large skillet over medium-high heat until hot but not smoking. Add chicken and cook 4 to 6 minutes per side, until golden brown on the outside and no longer pink in the center.

4. While chicken is cooking, bring water to a boil in a medium-size saucepan over high heat. Add cauliflower and broccoli and return water to a boil. Reduce heat to low; cover and cook 4 to 6 minutes, until vegetables are crisp-tender. Drain.

5. Add butter to saucepan and melt. Stir in basil and salt. Return vegetables to saucepan and toss to coat in butter.

6. Remove chicken to center of a heated platter. Arrange broccoli and cauliflower on platter. Spoon salsa over chicken and serve.

Makes 4 servings. Per serving: 379 calories, 35 grams protein, 20 grams carbohydrate, 18 grams fat, 151 milligrams cholesterol, 408 milligrams sodium

Chicken Breasts with Arugula Salsa, Broccoli and Cauliflower

Skillet Chicken and Red Rice

2 tablespoons vegetable oil
4 chicken-breast halves (about 8 ounces each)
1 cup uncooked long-grain white rice
1 medium-size green bell pepper, coarsely chopped
1 jar (about 15 ounces) marinara sauce
¾ cup water

1. Heat oil in a large skillet over high heat. Add chicken skin-side down and cook about 3 minutes, until skin is golden. Remove from skillet.

2. Add rice and bell pepper to skillet. Reduce heat to medium and cook 3 minutes, stirring constantly, until rice is lightly browned.

3. Stir in marinara sauce and water; bring to a boil.

4. Add chicken and reduce heat to low. Cover and simmer 40 minutes, until chicken and rice are tender. Transfer to a platter and serve.

Makes 4 servings. Per serving: 706 calories, 68 grams protein, 55 grams carbohydrate, 22 grams fat, 153 milligrams cholesterol, 827 milligrams sodium

Fruited Chicken Breasts

The flavors of chicken and fruit marry beautifully. The tang of citrus and the mellow sweetness of plums make these dishes special.

Stir-fried Chicken with Chiles and Oranges

Serve with a salad of shredded iceberg lettuce, sliced cucumber and tomato and avocado chunks tossed with Italian dressing. To cool palates, provide a refreshing pitcher of iced herbal tea with lime wedges. Instead of surrounding the chicken with tortilla chips, you can serve it over rice.

⅓ cup chicken broth or water
1½ tablespoons cider vinegar
1½ teaspoons all-purpose flour
 2 tablespoons olive or
    vegetable oil
 1 pound boned and skinned
    chicken-breast halves,
    cut in 1-inch chunks
 1 can (11 ounces) mandarin oranges,
    drained
 1 can (4 ounces) chopped green
    chiles, not drained
 1 tablespoon chopped fresh cilantro
    or 1 teaspoon dried cilantro
    leaves
 ¼ teaspoon salt
    Tortilla chips (optional)

1. Mix broth, vinegar and flour in a small cup until smooth.

2. Heat oil in a large heavy skillet over medium-high heat. Add chicken and stir-fry 2 to 3 minutes, until no longer pink.

3. Add broth mixture and cook 1 minute, stirring constantly, until sauce boils.

4. Add mandarin oranges, chiles, cilantro and salt. Simmer 1 minute, until chicken is cooked through, sauce has thickened slightly and some of the oranges have broken up.

5. Transfer chicken to a heated platter, surround with tortilla chips, if desired, and serve.

Makes 4 servings. Per serving (without chips): 209 calories, 23 grams protein, 8 grams carbohydrate, 9 grams fat, 57 milligrams cholesterol, 240 milligrams sodium

Chicken with Plums on Rice

The sweet tartness of the plums complements the chicken.

1½ cups water
 ½ teaspoon salt
1½ cups 5-minute rice
 1 tablespoon vegetable oil
 1 pound boned and skinned
    chicken-breast halves,
    cut in narrow strips
 ½ cup blanched slivered almonds
1½ cups frozen mixed vegetables
    (broccoli, green beans, pearl
    onions and red bell peppers) from
    a 16-ounce bag
 2 medium-size plums, halved, pitted
    and cut in thin wedges
 ¼ cup bottled Oriental plum sauce
    (see Note)
 ½ teaspoon Oriental sesame oil
    (see Note)

1. Bring water and salt to a boil in a medium-size covered saucepan over high heat. Stir in rice, cover, remove from heat and set aside.

2. Heat vegetable oil in a large skillet or wok over medium-high heat until hot but not smoking. Add chicken and almonds and stir-fry 3 minutes, until both are lightly browned.

3. Add frozen vegetables and stir-fry 2 minutes, until partially thawed.

4. Stir in plums, plum sauce and sesame oil and bring to a boil. Reduce heat to low and simmer 3 minutes, stirring once or twice, until vegetables are hot. Serve over the rice.

Makes 4 servings. Per serving: 397 calories, 28 grams protein, 40 grams carbohydrate, 14 grams fat, 56 milligrams cholesterol, 469 milligrams sodium

Note: Oriental plum sauce and sesame oil are available in the specialty- or international-foods section of most supermarkets. The sesame oil has a golden-brown color because it is made from toasted sesame seed. The oil is perishable, so keep it in a cool place or in the refrigerator. Sniff the oil before using to make sure it is fresh.

Stir-fried Chicken with Chiles and Oranges

Chicken with Plums on Rice

Lime Chicken

Lime juice and honey add a sweet-and-sour flavor to this colorful dish.

1½ cups chicken broth
1½ cups 5-minute rice
¼ cup all-purpose flour
1 teaspoon salt
¼ teaspoon pepper
1¼ pounds boned and skinned
    chicken-breast halves
6 tablespoons butter or margarine
2 tablespoons honey
1 large clove garlic, sliced
4 thin slices lime (cut 2 in half)
½ cup dry white wine
1 package (9 ounces) frozen Chinese
    pea pods
For garnish: roasted red peppers from a
    jar, drained and sliced, or fresh
    red bell pepper strips

1. Bring broth to a boil in a small saucepan over high heat. Stir in rice; remove from heat. Cover and set aside.

2. Mix flour, salt and pepper on a sheet of waxed paper. Coat chicken in flour mixture.

3. Melt 4 tablespoons of the butter with the honey, garlic and 2 of the whole slices lime in a large skillet over medium heat.

4. Add chicken and brown about 5 minutes, turning once.

5. Add remaining 2 tablespoons butter and the wine. Bring to a boil.

6. Add pea pods; reduce heat, cover and simmer 2 minutes, until pea pods are crisp-tender.

7. Remove to a heated serving platter. Garnish with remaining halved lime slices and red peppers. Serve with the rice.

Makes 4 servings. Per serving: 661 calories, 52 grams protein, 51 grams carbohydrate, 27 grams fat, 171 milligrams cholesterol with butter, 117 milligrams cholesterol with margarine, 1,119 milligrams sodium

Lime Chicken

Chicken and Squash with Orange Sauce

Buttered noodles and a spinach salad with red-onion rings are good accompaniments.

¾ cup orange juice
2 tablespoons orange marmalade
1½ teaspoons cornstarch
1 teaspoon grated fresh gingerroot
½ teaspoon Dijon mustard
2 tablespoons vegetable oil
1 pound boned and skinned chicken-breast halves, cut in 1-inch chunks
8 ounces yellow summer squash, cut in ¼-inch-thick rounds
8 ounces zucchini, cut in ¼-inch-thick rounds
½ teaspoon salt
Pepper to taste

1. Stir orange juice, marmalade, cornstarch, gingerroot and mustard in a small bowl until blended.

2. Heat oil in a large skillet or wok over medium-high heat until hot but not smoking. Add chicken and stir-fry 3 to 4 minutes, until no longer pink in the center. Remove with a slotted spoon to a platter.

3. Add yellow squash and zucchini to skillet and stir-fry until crisp-tender. Remove to same platter.

4. Stir juice mixture. Pour mixture into skillet and bring to a boil, stirring constantly, until sauce thickens and becomes clear.

5. Return chicken and vegetables to skillet and mix well with sauce. Add salt and pepper. Simmer just until chicken and vegetables are hot. Transfer to a heated platter and serve.

Makes 4 servings. Per serving: 246 calories, 24 grams protein, 17 grams carbohydrate, 9 grams fat, 56 milligrams cholesterol, 322 milligrams sodium

Orange-Chicken Pilaf

Serve this with a crisp green salad tossed with chick-peas, sliced olives and a garlic dressing. Before slicing the chicken, be sure to remove all the visible fat along the edges. The chicken will be easier to manage if you slice it while it is still cold. To remove chicken skin, grasp it with a paper towel and pull it and any underlying fat off.

1 tablespoon butter or margarine
1 pound boned and skinned chicken-breast halves, cut crosswise in narrow strips
2 cups sliced green onions
½ cup frozen mixed peas and carrots
1 cup orange juice, preferably fresh-squeezed
1 cup water
1 package (4.7 ounces) 10-minute almandine rice-and-sauce mix with vegetables
For garnish: lettuce leaves and thin orange wedges

1. Melt butter in a large skillet over medium-high heat. Add chicken and green onions. Increase heat to high and stir-fry 2 minutes, until chicken is lightly browned.

2. Stir in peas and carrots, orange juice, water and rice mix. Bring to a boil.

3. Reduce heat to low and simmer 8 to 10 minutes, stirring occasionally, until rice is tender.

4. Spoon onto a heated serving dish. Garnish with lettuce leaves and orange wedges and serve.

Makes 4 servings. Per serving: 399 calories, 41 grams protein, 35 grams carbohydrate, 10 grams fat, 99 milligrams cholesterol with butter, 90 milligrams cholesterol with margarine, 565 milligrams sodium

International Favorites

Feeling a little Italian this evening? Yearning for south-of-the-border spiciness? Or is French more your mood? Try the recipes that follow to give international flair to your dinner table.

Chicken Fajitas with Avocado Salad

Eat out-of-hand along with cucumber slices and cherry tomatoes. If you like, you can substitute shredded iceberg lettuce for the Boston.

Eight 7- to 8-inch flour tortillas
¼ cup all-purpose flour
½ teaspoon chili powder
¾ teaspoon salt
¼ teaspoon pepper
4 boned and skinned chicken-breast
    halves (about 4 ounces each)
2 tablespoons butter or margarine
1 ripe avocado, halved and pitted
1 fresh plum tomato, coarsely chopped
1 tablespoon lemon juice
8 Boston lettuce leaves
Salsa (optional)

1. Heat oven to 225°F.

2. Divide tortillas in two stacks. Wrap each stack in foil and place in oven to warm.

3. Put flour, chili powder, ¼ teaspoon of the salt and the pepper in a plastic food bag and shake to mix. Add chicken and shake to coat.

4. Melt butter in a large skillet over medium-high heat. Add chicken and cook 3 to 4 minutes per side, until golden brown and no longer pink in the center. Remove chicken to a cutting board.

5. While chicken cooks, spoon avocado from skin into a bowl and mash with a fork until chunky. Stir in tomato, lemon juice and remaining ½ teaspoon salt.

6. Cut chicken crosswise in narrow strips.

7. Unwrap tortillas and top each with a lettuce leaf. Arrange chicken strips in the center of each and spoon on avocado salad and salsa, if desired. Fold sides of tortillas over the filling. Transfer to heated plates and serve.

Makes 4 servings. Per serving (without salsa): 472 calories, 26 grams protein, 46 grams carbohydrate, 21 grams fat, 91 milligrams cholesterol with butter, 73 milligrams cholesterol with margarine, 479 milligrams sodium

Chicken Fajitas with Avocado Salad

♥ LOW-CALORIE

German Chicken

2 tablespoons vegetable oil
4 chicken-breast halves (about
    6 ounces each)
4 ounces smoked sausage, sliced
1½ cups chicken broth
½ cup packaged dry bread crumbs
¼ cup dry white wine
½ teaspoon salt
¼ teaspoon pepper

1. Heat oil in a large skillet over high heat. Add chicken and brown on both sides. Drain fat from skillet.

2. Add remaining ingredients and bring to a boil.

3. Reduce heat to low. Cover and simmer 30 minutes, until chicken is no longer pink in the center. Arrange chicken and sausage on a heated platter or plates and serve, or serve from skillet.

Makes 4 servings. Per serving: 295 calories, 24 grams protein, 10 grams carbohydrate, 18 grams fat, 67 milligrams cholesterol, 1,031 milligrams sodium

Persian Chicken with Chick-peas

Toasted pita wedges go well with this dish, or you can spoon it over rice.

3 tablespoons olive oil
1 medium-size red onion, thinly
    sliced (about 1 cup)
1½ pounds boned and skinned
    chicken-breast halves, cut in
    narrow strips
1 teaspoon ground cumin
¾ teaspoon salt
¼ teaspoon pepper
⅛ teaspoon ground cinnamon
½ cup dried apricot halves, each
    snipped in half
¼ cup golden raisins
1 small head escarole (about 8
    ounces), cut in 1-inch pieces
    (5½ cups loosely packed)
1 can (about 16 ounces) chick-peas,
    rinsed and drained
½ cup plain yogurt (optional)

1. Heat oil in a large, deep, heavy skillet over high heat. Add onion and cook 2 minutes, stirring occasionally, until limp.

2. Add chicken and season with cumin, salt, pepper and cinnamon. Stir to mix. Cook 3 to 4 minutes, turning chicken strips often, until no longer pink.

3. Stir apricots and raisins into skillet. Add escarole in two batches, stirring well after each, until escarole is well coated.

4. Stir in chick-peas. Cover and cook 2 to 3 minutes, until escarole is wilted and chick-peas are hot.

5. Transfer to plates and top each serving with yogurt, if desired.

Makes 4 servings. Per serving (without yogurt): 465 calories, 37 grams protein, 44 grams carbohydrate, 16 grams fat, 86 milligrams cholesterol, 420 milligrams sodium

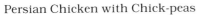

Persian Chicken with Chick-peas

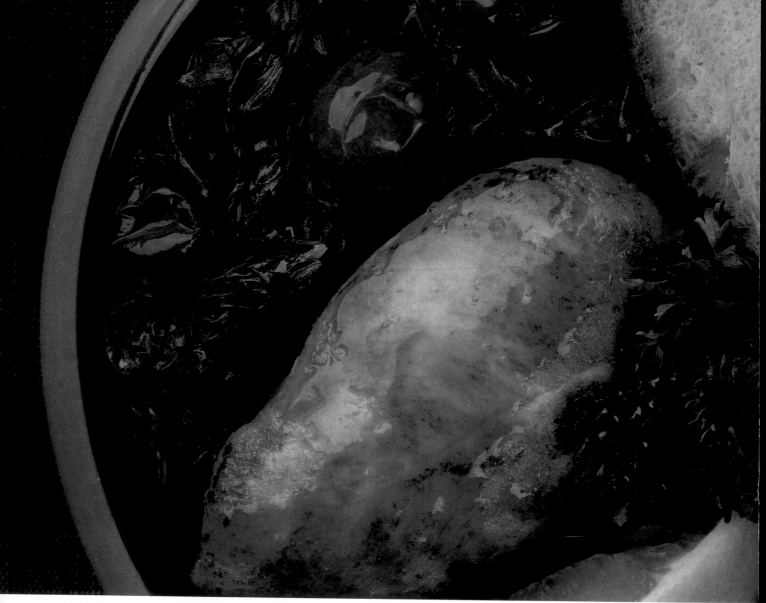

Chicken Piccata with Vegetables

Chicken Piccata with Vegetables

For dessert, top scoops of lemon sherbet with sliced, sugared strawberries or raspberries.

  4 **boned and skinned chicken-breast
       halves (about 5 ounces each)**
  ¼ **teaspoon salt**
  ¼ **teaspoon pepper**
  2 **tablespoons olive oil**
  ½ **cup water**
  1 **chicken-bouillon cube or 1
       teaspoon instant broth granules**
  4 **teaspoons lemon juice**
  1 **tablespoon butter or margarine**
  1 **bag (10 to 12 ounces) fresh spinach,
       trimmed, rinsed and well drained**
12 **cherry tomatoes**

1. Season chicken with salt and pepper.

2. Heat oil in a large skillet over high heat until hot but not smoking. Add chicken and cook 3 to 4 minutes per side, until browned and no longer pink in the center.

3. Carefully add water and bouillon to skillet. Cook 1 minute, stirring to loosen browned bits on bottom of skillet.

4. Remove chicken to a heated platter.

5. Add lemon juice and butter to skillet and stir until butter melts. Pour sauce over chicken.

6. Add spinach and tomatoes to skillet. Cook 2 to 3 minutes, stirring constantly, until spinach wilts and tomatoes are hot. Serve vegetables with chicken.

Makes 4 servings. Per serving: 380 calories, 48 grams protein, 12 grams carbohydrate, 15 grams fat, 122 milligrams cholesterol with butter, 113 milligrams cholesterol with margarine, 555 milligrams sodium

Chicken Tetrazzini with Rice

This dish, named after famous singer Luisa Tetrazzini, can be made with turkey, too. A Caesar salad is a good accompaniment.

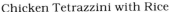

- 2 cups chicken broth
- 1½ cups 5-minute rice
- 1 tablespoon olive oil
- 1 pound boned and skinned chicken-breast halves, cut crosswise in narrow strips
- ¼ teaspoon salt
- ¼ teaspoon pepper
- ¼ teaspoon paprika
- 1 small green bell pepper, cut in strips
- ½ cup frozen or fresh chopped onion
- ½ teaspoon minced fresh garlic
- 1 jar (4 ounces) sliced pimientos, drained
- 1 jar (4½ ounces) sliced mushrooms, drained

1. Bring 1½ cups of the broth to a boil in a medium-size saucepan over high heat. Stir in rice, cover, remove from heat and set aside.

2. Heat oil in a large skillet over medium-high heat. Add chicken; season with salt, pepper and paprika.

3. Add bell pepper, onion and garlic and stir-fry 3 to 4 minutes, until chicken is golden brown and vegetables are crisp-tender.

4. Stir in pimientos, mushrooms and remaining ½ cup broth. Bring to a boil, reduce heat to low and simmer about 2 minutes. Serve over the rice.

Makes 4 servings. Per serving: 321 calories, 31 grams protein, 34 grams carbohydrate, 6 grams fat, 66 milligrams cholesterol, 793 milligrams sodium

Chicken Tetrazzini with Rice

Chicken Strips Mediterranean-Style

Roasted red peppers from a jar can be substituted for the pimientos. If you can't find oil-cured olives, substitute Greek calamata olives or ripe olives from California.

- 2 tablespoons all-purpose flour
- ½ teaspoon salt
- ¼ teaspoon pepper
- 1¼ pounds boned and skinned chicken-breast halves, cut crosswise in ¾-inch-thick strips
- 2 tablespoons vegetable oil
- ½ cup dry white wine or chicken broth
- ½ cup half-and-half
- 1 jar (4 ounces) pimientos, drained and diced
- ¼ cup pitted oil-cured black olives (optional)
- 1 cup diagonally sliced green onions

1. Mix flour, salt and pepper on a sheet of waxed paper. Coat chicken in flour mixture.

2. Heat oil in a large skillet over high heat. Add chicken strips and cook, stirring constantly, until browned. Remove chicken to a platter.

3. Add wine, half-and-half, pimientos and olives, if desired, to skillet. Simmer over medium-high heat about 5 minutes, stirring frequently, until sauce is slightly thickened.

4. Return chicken to skillet. Add green onions and simmer until hot. Transfer to a heated platter and serve.

Makes 4 servings. Per serving (with wine, without olives): 350 calories, 41 grams protein, 9 grams carbohydrate, 15 grams fat, 111 milligrams cholesterol, 369 milligrams sodium

♥ LOW-CALORIE
Provençale Chicken Skillet

- 2 tablespoons vegetable oil
- 1 pound boned and skinned chicken-breast halves, cut in ½-inch chunks, patted dry
- 2 large stalks celery, cut in thin slices
- 1 large green bell pepper, cut in thin strips
- 1 medium-size onion, chopped
- 1 teaspoon salt
- ½ teaspoon minced fresh garlic
- ½ teaspoon dried marjoram leaves
- 2 medium-size fresh tomatoes, cut in 1-inch chunks (about 2 cups)

1. Heat oil in a large skillet over medium-high heat until hot but not smoking. Add chicken and cook 3 minutes, turning frequently, until lightly browned.

2. Add remaining ingredients except tomatoes. Cook about 5 minutes, stirring frequently, until vegetables are crisp-tender.

3. Stir in tomatoes and cook 2 minutes, until hot. Transfer to a heated serving dish.

Makes 4 servings. Per serving: 217 calories, 24 grams protein, 9 grams carbohydrate, 10 grams fat, 7 milligrams cholesterol, 613 milligrams sodium

♥ LOW-CALORIE
Chicken Stroganoff

To save time, look for presliced stir-fry chicken strips available at the meat counter in many supermarkets.

- 3 teaspoons butter or margarine
- 2 tablespoons chopped onion
- 1 pound boned and skinned chicken-breast halves, cut in ½-inch strips
- 8 ounces mushrooms, sliced (about 3 cups)
- ¼ cup chicken broth
- ¼ cup dry white wine
- ¼ teaspoon *each* salt, pepper and dried thyme leaves
- ¼ cup sour cream

1. Melt 2 teaspoons of the butter in a large skillet over medium-high heat. Add onion and cook 2 minutes, stirring constantly.

2. Add chicken and cook 2 to 3 minutes, stirring constantly, until browned. Remove chicken from skillet.

3. Melt remaining 1 teaspoon butter in skillet. Add mushrooms and cook 2 minutes, stirring constantly.

4. Add broth, wine, salt, pepper and thyme. Reduce heat to medium-low and simmer 7 to 10 minutes, until mushrooms are tender and juices are slightly reduced.

5. Return chicken to skillet. Stir until hot; stir in sour cream. Transfer to a heated platter and serve.

Makes 4 servings. Per serving: 229 calories, 29 grams protein, 4 grams carbohydrate, 9 grams fat, 83 milligrams cholesterol with butter, 74 milligrams cholesterol with margarine, 285 milligrams sodium

Easy Elegance with Chicken Cutlets

★ SPECIAL—AND WORTH IT

Chicken Breasts Stuffed with Swiss Chard

You can substitute spinach for the chard.

5 tablespoons olive oil
⅓ cup finely chopped onion
¾ teaspoon minced fresh garlic
8 ounces Swiss chard; remove tough
    stems and chop leaves and tender
    stems (2 cups)
¾ teaspoon salt
⅛ teaspoon pepper
3 tablespoons toasted pignoli
    (pine nuts)
3 tablespoons golden raisins
4 boned and skinned chicken-breast
    halves (about 5 ounces each)
¼ cup all-purpose flour
1 tablespoon chopped fresh parsley

1. Heat 3 tablespoons of the oil in a large skillet over medium heat. Add onion and garlic and cook 3 to 4 minutes, stirring frequently, until wilted.

2. Add chard, salt and pepper and cook 5 minutes, stirring often, until chard is wilted. Remove from heat and add 2 tablespoons each of the pine nuts and raisins. Transfer mixture to a bowl to cool.

3. Remove the small strip of meat (filet) from the underside of each chicken-breast half. Flatten each strip with fingers until about 2 inches wide at widest point. Cut a lengthwise slit in underside of each breast to form a pocket. Fill each with ¼ of the chard mixture. Cover stuffing with flattened strips of chicken.

4. Coat chicken in flour.

5. Heat remaining 2 tablespoons oil in skillet over medium-high heat. Add chicken and cook 2 to 3 minutes per side, until golden brown and fork-tender. Remove to a heated platter.

6. Add remaining pine nuts, raisins and the parsley to skillet. Stir in pan juices, then spoon over chicken to coat.

Makes 4 servings. Per serving: 456 calories, 42 grams protein, 15 grams carbohydrate, 26 grams fat, 90 milligrams cholesterol, 560 milligrams sodium

Stuffing a Chicken Breast

Cut a skinned and boned chicken breast in two. Remove the white tendon from the bottom of each half.

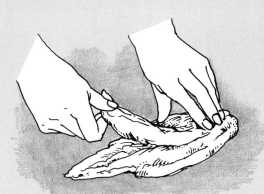

Remove the small strip of meat (filet) from the underside of each chicken-breast half.

Flatten each strip with fingers until about 2 inches wide at widest point.

Cut a lengthwise slit in underside of each breast to form a pocket. Fill each with stuffing and cover with flattened strips of chicken.

Rosemary-Orange Chicken with Fresh Spinach

Rosemary-Orange Dressing (recipe
     follows)
  4 boned and skinned chicken-breast
     halves (about 4 ounces each),
     flattened (see Flattening Chicken
     Breasts, page 23)
  ¼ teaspoon salt
  ¼ teaspoon pepper
1½ tablespoons olive or vegetable oil
12 ounces fresh spinach, washed,
     drained and thick stems removed
     (8 cups loosely packed leaves)
  2 large navel oranges, peeled (with
     white membrane removed) and
     each cut in 8 rounds
  4 ounces seedless green grapes,
     halved (¾ cup)

1. Prepare Rosemary-Orange Dressing.

2. Season chicken with salt and pepper.

3. Heat oil in a large nonstick skillet over medium heat until oil is hot but not smoking. Add chicken and cook about 2 minutes per side, until golden brown on the outside and the pink color is almost gone in the center. Remove to a cutting board. Cover with foil and let stand about 3 minutes.

4. Meanwhile, toss spinach with ¼ cup of the dressing in a large bowl. Arrange on four plates.

5. Slice chicken crosswise in ½-inch-wide slices. Arrange over spinach and sprinkle with the carving juices. Garnish with oranges and grapes. Pour remaining dressing over chicken and fruit and serve.

Makes 4 servings. Per serving: 318 calories, 26 grams protein, 7 grams carbohydrate, 21 grams fat, 56 milligrams cholesterol, 656 milligrams sodium

Rosemary-Orange Dressing

⅓ cup fresh-squeezed orange juice
  2 tablespoons red-wine vinegar
  1 teaspoon granulated sugar
  ¾ teaspoon salt
  ¾ teaspoon crumbled dried
     rosemary leaves
  ½ teaspoon lemon juice
  ¼ teaspoon pepper
  4 drops hot-pepper sauce
  ¼ cup olive or vegetable oil

Whisk orange juice, vinegar, sugar, salt, rosemary, lemon juice, pepper and hot-pepper sauce in a small bowl. Gradually beat in oil.

Makes ⅔ cup.

Rosemary-Orange Chicken with Fresh Spinach

Garlic-Lemon Chicken Breasts

For best flavor, use really fresh garlic. Serve this main dish with lightly buttered, steamed fresh spinach and white rice or crusty whole-grain bread.

  4 boned and skinned chicken-breast
     halves (about 4 ounces each),
     flattened (see Flattening Chicken
     Breasts, page 23)
  ¼ teaspoon salt
  ¼ teaspoon pepper
  2 tablespoons butter or margarine
  ⅓ cup dry white wine (optional)
  ½ teaspoon minced fresh garlic
  4 thin slices lemon
  1 to 2 teaspoons lemon juice

1. Season chicken with salt and pepper.

2. Heat 1 tablespoon of the butter in a large nonstick skillet over medium heat until it foams. Add chicken and cook about 2 minutes per side, until golden brown on the outside and the pink color is almost gone in the center. Remove to a heated platter.

3. Add wine to skillet, if desired, and raise heat to high. Boil about 2 minutes, until liquid is reduced to 3 tablespoons. (If not using wine, omit this step.)

4. Reduce heat to low and add remaining 1 tablespoon butter, the garlic and lemon slices. Heat about 30 seconds, stirring gently, until butter has melted and lemon slices have browned slightly.

5. Remove from heat. Stir lemon juice into skillet and spoon sauce over chicken breasts. Top each chicken breast with a slice of lemon and serve.

Makes 4 servings. Per serving (with wine): 167 calories, 22 grams protein, 0 grams carbohydrate, 8 grams fat, 74 milligrams cholesterol with butter, 56 milligrams cholesterol with margarine, 248 milligrams sodium

---

Perfect Cooking

The secret to preparing juicy, tender chicken breasts is to undercook them ever so slightly. The chicken will continue cooking after it is removed from the skillet if it is covered or removed to a hot platter while you are completing the recipe or making the sauce.

Chicken in Tarragon Cream

You can trim calories by making the lower-fat variation that follows. Good accompaniments: steamed broccoli, and rice sprinkled with grated lemon peel.

  4 boned and skinned chicken-breast halves (about 4 ounces each), flattened (see Flattening Chicken Breasts, page 23)
½ teaspoon *each* salt and pepper
2½ tablespoons minced fresh tarragon leaves or 1½ teaspoons dried tarragon leaves, crumbled
  1 tablespoon butter or margarine
  1 cup heavy cream
  1 teaspoon lemon juice
For garnish: fresh tarragon or parsley sprigs

1. Season chicken with ¼ teaspoon each of the salt and pepper. Sprinkle with tarragon.

2. Heat butter in a large skillet over medium heat until it foams. Add chicken and cook about 2 minutes per side, until golden brown on the outside and the pink color is almost gone in the center. Remove to a heated platter.

3. Add cream to skillet and bring to a boil. Simmer about 4 minutes, stirring often, until cream has thickened and is reduced to about ⅔ cup.

4. Stir in lemon juice and remaining ¼ teaspoon each salt and pepper. Pour sauce over chicken. Garnish with tarragon sprigs and serve.

Makes 4 servings. Per serving: 351 calories, 23 grams protein, 2 grams carbohydrate, 28 grams fat, 144 milligrams cholesterol with butter, 135 milligrams cholesterol with margarine, 365 milligrams sodium

Lower-Calorie Variation: Use only ½ cup heavy cream instead of 1 cup. Pour into skillet as directed and simmer 2 to 3 minutes, stirring often, until cream has thickened and is reduced to about ⅓ cup. Remove skillet from heat. Stir in ⅓ cup plain yogurt until well blended. Omit lemon juice and add remaining salt and pepper as directed. Pour the sauce over chicken.

Makes 4 servings. Per serving: 261 calories, 23 grams protein, 4 grams carbohydrate, 17 grams fat, 108 milligrams cholesterol with butter, 99 milligrams cholesterol with margarine, 414 milligrams sodium

Chicken in Tarragon Cream

Chicken in Raspberry Sauce

Serve with buttered baby carrots and rice sprinkled with lightly toasted slivered almonds. Sliced pound cake topped with hot-fudge sauce would make a good dessert.

2 tablespoons butter or margarine
6 boned and skinned chicken-breast halves (about 6 ounces each)
1 package (about 1 ounce; 1-cup yield) white-sauce mix
1 cup cranberry-raspberry drink
½ cup frozen unsweetened red raspberries, thawed and mashed
2 tablespoons dry red wine (optional)
For garnish: fresh dill sprigs

1. Melt butter in a large heavy skillet over medium-high heat. Add chicken and brown lightly on both sides.

2. Reduce heat to low. Cover and cook 15 minutes, until chicken is no longer pink in the center. Remove chicken to a cutting board or a plate; cover and keep warm. Measure ¼ cup chicken drippings from the skillet and reserve.

3. Stir white-sauce mix and cranberry-raspberry drink in a small saucepan until smooth. Cook over medium heat, stirring occasionally, until sauce starts to thicken. Stir in raspberries, wine, if desired, and reserved chicken drippings and bring to a boil. Remove from heat.

4. To serve, cut chicken in ⅛-inch-thick slices. Pour sauce onto a heated serving platter and arrange chicken over sauce. Garnish with dill sprigs and serve.

Makes 6 servings. Per serving (with wine): 394 calories, 54 grams protein, 13 grams carbohydrate, 12 grams fat, 146 milligrams cholesterol with butter, 134 milligrams cholesterol with margarine, 261 milligrams sodium

Flattening Chicken Breasts

Pat chicken dry with paper towels. Place each boned and skinned chicken-breast half between two sheets of waxed paper and pound gently with a meat mallet, the flat side of a cleaver or the bottom of a heavy pan or skillet until about ⅝-inch thick.

Boning a Chicken Breast

Lay breast skin side down; run knife down center of breast to sever membrane and expose keel bone (spoon-shaped bone).

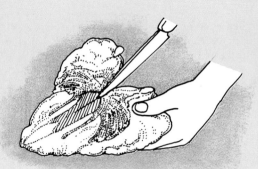

Put a thumb on tip end of keel bone, other at base of rib cage, grasp breast in both hands. Bend it back until keel bone breaks through.

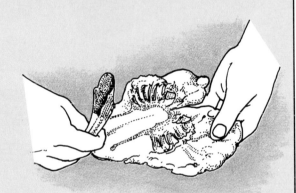

Run finger under edges of keel bone and thick cartilage to loosen then pull bone out.

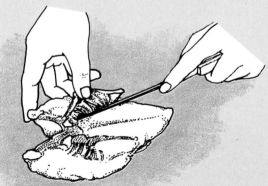

Poke knife under long first rib. Rest it against bones; scrape meat away from bones. Cut ribs off; sever and remove shoulder joint. Repeat on other side. Cut out wishbone at top of breast. Cut breast in half along the natural separation; remove any remaining cartilage. If desired, pull off skin and fat.

Almond-Cascade Chicken

★ SPECIAL—AND WORTH IT
Almond-Cascade Chicken

This is delicious with boiled new potatoes.

---

4 **boned and skinned chicken-breast halves (about 4 ounces each), flattened (see Flattening Chicken Breasts, page 23)**
½ **teaspoon *each* salt and pepper**
1 **tablespoon butter or margarine**
½ **cup dry white wine (optional)**
1 **cup heavy cream**
1 **teaspoon fresh-squeezed lemon juice**
½ **cup (2 ounces) toasted, chopped unblanched almonds (see Toasting Nuts, page 25)**
¼ **cup chopped watercress leaves or 2 tablespoons finely chopped fresh parsley**
For garnish: watercress sprigs, cherry tomatoes or small pear tomatoes

1. Season chicken with ¼ teaspoon each of the salt and pepper.

2. Heat butter in a large nonstick skillet over medium heat until it foams. Add chicken and cook about 2 minutes per side, until golden brown on the outside and the pink color is almost gone in the center. Remove to a heated platter.

3. Add wine to skillet, if desired. Raise heat to high and boil about 3 minutes, until liquid is reduced to about 2 tablespoons. (If not using wine, omit this step.)

4. Add cream and bring to a boil. Reduce heat to medium. Cook about 4 minutes, stirring often, until cream has thickened and is reduced to about ⅔ cup. Remove from heat.

5. Stir in lemon juice and remaining ¼ teaspoon each salt and pepper. Pour sauce over chicken. Sprinkle with almonds and chopped watercress. Garnish with watercress sprigs and tomatoes and serve.

Makes 4 servings. Per serving (with wine): 449 calories, 27 grams protein, 5 grams carbohydrate, 36 grams fat, 144 milligrams cholesterol with butter, 135 milligrams cholesterol with margarine, 367 milligrams sodium

Hazelnut-Apricot Chicken Breasts

This is wonderful with hot, buttered corn bread, and fresh spinach.

½ cup dried apricot halves
¼ cup water
½ teaspoon granulated sugar
1¼ teaspoons dried thyme leaves, crumbled
⅛ teaspoon plus ½ teaspoon dried marjoram leaves, crumbled
4 boned and skinned chicken-breast halves (about 4 ounces each), flattened (see Flattening Chicken Breasts, page 23)
¼ teaspoon salt
¼ teaspoon pepper
2 tablespoons butter or margarine
⅓ cup finely chopped onion
1 tablespoon lemon juice
⅓ cup coarsely chopped toasted hazelnuts (see Toasting Nuts, below)
For garnish: lemon wedges

1. Put apricots and water in a small saucepan. Bring to a boil over high heat. Reduce heat to medium-low and simmer 5 minutes, stirring occasionally, just until tender. Remove from heat and drain well. Return drained apricots to saucepan.

2. Stir sugar, ¼ teaspoon of the thyme and ⅛ teaspoon of the marjoram into apricots.

3. Season chicken with salt, pepper and remaining thyme and marjoram.

4. Heat 1 tablespoon of the butter in a large nonstick skillet over medium heat until it foams. Add chicken and cook about 2 minutes per side, until golden brown on the outside and the pink color is almost gone in the center. Remove to a heated platter.

5. Melt remaining 1 tablespoon butter in skillet. Add onion and cook 2 minutes, stirring often, until onion is tender and golden.

6. Stir in apricot mixture and lemon juice and cook just until hot. Spoon alongside and slightly over chicken breasts. Sprinkle with hazelnuts. Garnish with lemon wedges and serve.

Makes 4 servings. Per serving: 279 calories, 24 grams protein, 15 grams carbohydrate, 14 grams fat, 74 milligrams cholesterol with butter, 56 milligrams cholesterol with margarine, 254 milligrams sodium

Chicken Cutlets with Cucumbers and Dill

Use a teaspoon, a long-handled iced-tea spoon or a melon-baller to remove the seeds from the cucumber.

3 tablespoons butter or margarine
4 boned and skinned chicken-breast halves (about 5 ounces each), pounded ¼ inch thick (see Flattening Chicken Breasts, page 23)
½ teaspoon salt
Pepper to taste
1 medium-size cucumber, peeled, halved lengthwise, seeded and sliced ¼ inch thick (about 2½ cups)
2 teaspoons minced fresh dill or ½ teaspoon dried dillweed
3 tablespoons lemon juice

1. Melt 2 tablespoons of the butter in a large skillet over medium heat. Add chicken and cook 3 minutes per side, until lightly browned on the outside and no longer pink in the center. Season with salt and pepper. Remove to a heated platter and keep warm.

2. Melt remaining 1 tablespoon butter in skillet. Add cucumber and dill and cook about 3 minutes, stirring occasionally, until cucumber is crisp-tender. Remove cucumber from skillet with a slotted spoon and arrange around chicken.

3. Add lemon juice to skillet, bring to a boil and cook about 1 minute, until slightly reduced. Spoon juices over chicken and serve.

Makes 4 servings. Per serving: 220 calories, 25 grams protein, 3 grams carbohydrate, 11 grams fat, 89 milligrams cholesterol with butter, 62 milligrams cholesterol with margarine, 427 milligrams sodium

---

Toasting Nuts

To toast almonds or hazelnuts, cook 4 to 5 minutes in a small nonstick skillet over medium heat, tossing often, until golden brown. Or toast in a small baking dish in a microwave oven until golden brown.

Chicken with Red Peppers

The peppers may be roasted and peeled as early as two days ahead. Serve this dish with angel-hair pasta or thin spaghetti tossed with olive oil and Parmesan cheese.

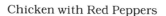

- 4 **boned and skinned chicken-breast halves (about 4 ounces each), flattened (see Flattening Chicken Breasts, page 23)**
- ½ **teaspoon salt**
- ¼ **teaspoon pepper**
- 1½ **tablespoons olive oil**
- 4 **large red bell peppers, roasted (see Note), or 2 jars (7 ounces each) roasted red peppers, drained and cut in ¼-inch-wide strips**
- 2 **teaspoons minced fresh garlic**
- 3 **tablespoons white-wine vinegar or rice-wine vinegar**
- 1 **teaspoon finely chopped fresh parsley**

For garnish: fresh parsley sprigs

1. Season chicken with ¼ teaspoon of the salt and the pepper.

2. Heat oil in a large nonstick skillet over medium heat until hot but not smoking. Add chicken and cook about 2 minutes per side, until golden brown on the outside and the pink color is almost gone in the center. Remove to a cutting board. Cover with foil to keep warm and let stand about 2 minutes.

3. Reduce heat under skillet to low. Add pepper strips, garlic, vinegar and remaining ¼ teaspoon salt to skillet. Stir gently and cook just until hot.

4. Slice chicken crosswise into ¼-inch-thick slices. Arrange on a heated platter and sprinkle with the carving juices. Remove peppers with a slotted spoon and arrange alongside chicken; spoon pan juices over top. Sprinkle with chopped parsley; garnish with parsley sprigs and serve.

Makes 4 servings. Per serving: 214 calories, 24 grams protein, 12 grams carbohydrate, 8 grams fat, 56 milligrams cholesterol, 333 milligrams sodium

Note: To roast the red peppers, arrange on foil-lined broiler-pan rack. Broil 2 inches from heat source, turning often, until well blistered and charred on all sides. Put peppers in a bowl and cover tightly with foil, or put them in a paper bag and close bag tightly. Cool. Working over a strainer in the sink, peel off skins. Remove stems, seeds and membranes. Cut peppers in ¼-inch-wide strips. If you have a gas stove, char peppers directly over the high flames of the burners. Turn often with tongs to blister peppers evenly.

Chicken with Red Peppers

Herb-Prosciutto Chicken

★ **SPECIAL—AND WORTH IT**
♥ **LOW-CALORIE**

Herb-Prosciutto Chicken

Serve with buttered peas. In season, go to the trouble of shelling and cooking fresh peas. They are delicious cooked French-style: Simmer peas just until tender in a little chicken broth or water, with some small tender lettuce leaves, the sliced white parts of green onions and a few sliced or quartered mushrooms. Season to taste with salt and pepper.

> 4 **boned and skinned chicken-breast halves (about 4 ounces each), flattened (see Flattening Chicken Breasts, page 23)**
> 2 **teaspoons snipped fresh chives (optional)**
> ½ **to 1 teaspoon dried tarragon leaves, crumbled**
> ¼ **teaspoon salt**
> ¼ **teaspoon pepper**
> 2 **tablespoons butter or margarine**
> 1½ **tablespoons finely chopped fresh parsley**
> 2 **ounces thinly sliced prosciutto ham (about 4 slices), trimmed**
> 2 **teaspoons fresh lemon juice**
> **For garnish: lemon slices or wedges**

1. Season chicken with chives, if desired, tarragon, salt and pepper, lightly pressing herbs onto surface so that they cling.

2. Heat butter in a large nonstick skillet over medium heat until it foams. Add chicken and cook about 2 minutes per side, until golden brown on the outside and the pink color is almost gone in the center. Remove chicken to a heated platter and sprinkle with parsley.

3. Increase heat under skillet to high. Add prosciutto and cook quickly until slices are frizzled. Remove prosciutto to paper towels to drain and remove skillet from heat.

4. Stir lemon juice into skillet. Spoon juices over chicken.

5. Tear prosciutto into ½-inch pieces and sprinkle over chicken. Garnish with lemon slices or wedges and serve.

Makes 4 servings. Per serving: 208 calories, 25 grams protein, 1 gram carbohydrate, 11 grams fat, 81 milligrams cholesterol with butter, 63 milligrams cholesterol with margarine, 375 milligrams sodium

Chicken with Tomato-Olive Sauce

Serve with crusty bread.

---

    4 boned and skinned chicken-breast
        halves (about 4 ounces each),
        flattened (see Flattening Chicken
        Breasts, page 23)
    1 teaspoon pepper
    ½ teaspoon salt
    ½ teaspoon crumbled dried
        thyme leaves
    1½ teaspoons snipped fresh
        or ¼ teaspoon crumbled dried
        rosemary leaves
    3 tablespoons olive oil
Tomato-Olive Sauce (recipe follows)
For garnish: fresh rosemary sprigs
        or parsley

1. Season chicken with pepper, salt, thyme and rosemary.

2. Heat oil in a large heavy skillet over medium heat. Add chicken and cook about 3 minutes per side, until no longer pink in the center.

3. Remove chicken to heated dinner plates. Spoon ¼ of the Tomato-Olive Sauce alongside each. Garnish with rosemary sprigs and serve.

Makes 4 servings. Per serving: 356 calories, 23 grams protein, 6 grams carbohydrate, 27 grams fat, 56 milligrams cholesterol, 477 milligrams sodium

Tomato-Olive Sauce

    ⅓ cup chopped onion
    ¼ cup olive oil
    1 tablespoon minced fresh garlic
    1 can (28 ounces) tomatoes,
        preferably imported Italian,
        drained, seeded, if desired, and
        chopped; or 2 cups chopped,
        seeded, peeled fresh tomatoes
    2 large bay leaves
    ¼ teaspoon *each* salt and granulated
        sugar
    ⅛ teaspoon pepper
    20 pitted ripe olives

1. Cook onion in oil in a medium skillet over medium heat about 3 minutes, until tender.

2. Stir in garlic, tomatoes and bay leaves. Simmer 25 minutes, stirring occasionally, until thick.

3. Add remaining ingredients and simmer 10 minutes longer to blend flavors. Discard bay leaves.

Makes about 1⅓ cups.

Chicken with Tomato-Olive Sauce

Chicken and Avocado in Cream

Serve this elegant dish with steamed white rice and thin green beans or fresh pencil-thin asparagus spears.

    1½ pounds boned and skinned
        chicken-breast halves, cut
        lengthwise in narrow strips
    ½ teaspoon salt
Pepper to taste
    2 tablespoons butter or margarine
    1 tablespoon minced shallot or white
        part of green onion
    4 ounces mushrooms, sliced (about
        1¼ cups)
    2 tablespoons cognac or brandy
        (optional)
    1½ cups heavy cream or half-and-half
    1 medium-size avocado, halved,
        pitted, peeled and cut lengthwise
        in 12 slices

1. Season chicken with salt and pepper.

2. Melt butter in a large heavy skillet over high heat. Add chicken strips and stir-fry 3 to 4 minutes, until no longer pink. Remove chicken to a plate with a slotted spoon.

3. Add shallot and mushrooms to skillet. Cook, stirring often, until mushrooms brown slightly.

4. Sprinkle mushrooms with cognac, if desired, making sure to keep your face well away from skillet in case the cognac ignites. Pour in cream, reduce heat to medium and simmer about 5 minutes, until sauce is reduced by about half and is thick enough to coat a spoon.

5. Return chicken to skillet and heat through. Add avocado slices and stir gently, just until warm. Arrange on a heated platter and serve.

Makes 4 servings. Per serving (with heavy cream): 642 calories, 37 grams protein, 8 grams carbohydrate, 52 grams fat, 220 milligrams cholesterol with butter, 202 milligrams cholesterol with margarine, 439 milligrams sodium

Artichoke and Chicken Sauté

Serve with corn bread and a green salad tossed with vinaigrette dressing, small chunks of blue cheese and toasted walnuts. For a very festive look, use both yellow and red bell peppers in this dish and sprinkle with coarsely chopped fresh cilantro or flat-leaf Italian parsley. Sliced fresh strawberries topped with vanilla yogurt make a simple but special dessert.

- 3 strips bacon, cut in ½-inch pieces
- 1¼ pounds boned and skinned chicken-breast halves, cut in 1-inch pieces
- 1 medium-size (6 ounces) red bell pepper, cut in thin strips
- 1 can (14 ounces) artichoke hearts, drained and quartered
- ¼ cup thinly sliced green onions
- ¼ teaspoon ground coriander seed or ⅛ teaspoon ground nutmeg
- ¼ teaspoon salt

1. Fry bacon in a large skillet over medium-high heat until crisp. Remove to paper towels to drain. Drain off all but 1 tablespoon bacon drippings.

2. Add chicken pieces to skillet and cook 3 minutes, stirring often, until no longer pink.

3. Add bell pepper and cook 3 minutes, stirring constantly, until crisp-tender.

4. Add artichokes, green onions, coriander and salt and cook about 2 minutes, stirring frequently, until artichokes are hot. Transfer to a heated platter and serve.

Makes 4 servings. Per serving: 291 calories, 47 grams protein, 5 grams carbohydrate, 8 grams fat, 117 milligrams cholesterol, 442 milligrams sodium

Oat and Sesame Chicken

The chicken is coated with a crunchy and nutritious mixture of oat bran and sesame seed. After dipping breasts in oat mixture, let them stand 5 to 10 minutes (or refrigerate them for several hours) before cooking; the coating will adhere better.

- 1 cup uncooked oat bran
- ½ cup sesame seed
- 2 teaspoons paprika
- ½ teaspoon salt
- ¼ teaspoon pepper
- Whites from 2 large eggs
- ¼ cup buttermilk
- 6 boned and skinned chicken-breast halves (about 2 pounds)
- 4 tablespoons olive oil

1. Mix oat bran, sesame seed, paprika, salt and pepper on a sheet of waxed paper.

2. Beat egg whites and buttermilk in a pie plate with a fork until blended.

3. Dip chicken in egg mixture, then coat in oat-bran mixture, pressing coating firmly onto chicken. (All coating mixture should be used.) Let stand 5 to 10 minutes or refrigerate for up to 3 hours.

4. Heat 2 tablespoons of the oil in a large skillet over medium-high heat. Add chicken and cook about 3 minutes. Turn chicken over and add remaining 2 tablespoons oil to skillet, tilting pan to distribute oil evenly. Cook another 2 to 3 minutes, until chicken feels springy when pressed and is no longer pink in the center. Transfer to a heated platter and serve.

Makes 6 servings. Per serving: 436 calories, 53 grams protein, 11 grams carbohydrate, 19 grams fat, 120 milligrams cholesterol, 313 milligrams sodium

Creamed Cider Chicken

Serve with boiled tiny potatoes tossed in butter and a Boston lettuce and avocado salad dressed with olive oil and lemon juice. Orange or lemon sherbet and crisp cookies would be a refreshing finish to the meal.

> 6 **boned and skinned chicken-breast halves (about 5 ounces each)**
> 2 **cups thinly sliced onions**
> 1 **cup apple cider**
> ½ **cup chicken broth**
> ¼ **cup applejack brandy or additional apple cider**
> 1½ **cups heavy cream**
> ½ **teaspoon salt, or to taste**
> ¼ **teaspoon pepper**
> 2 **tablespoons chopped almonds**
> 2 **tablespoons thinly sliced green onions**
> 2 **tablespoons chopped mushrooms**
> 2 **tablespoons chopped fresh parsley**

1. Put chicken in a large heavy skillet. Sprinkle onions over chicken and pour in cider and broth. Bring liquid to a boil over medium-high heat.

2. Reduce heat to medium-low. Cover and simmer 15 to 20 minutes, until chicken is fork-tender.

3. Remove chicken to a heated platter; cover tightly and keep warm.

4. Add applejack to skillet. Increase heat to high and boil 5 to 8 minutes, until liquid is reduced to about ½ cup.

5. Add cream and boil 3 to 5 minutes longer, until sauce coats a spoon and is reduced to about 1 cup. Season with salt and pepper.

6. Drain off and discard juices that have accumulated on platter.

7. Pour sauce through a strainer over chicken breasts. Sprinkle almonds, green onions, mushrooms and parsley over top and serve.

Makes 6 servings. Per serving (with applejack): 519 calories, 50 grams protein, 12 grams carbohydrate, 29 grams fat, 200 milligrams cholesterol, 359 milligrams sodium

Spicy Herbed-Peppercorn Chicken Breasts

This would be good served with fresh green beans, cooked crisp-tender and tossed in a skillet with olive oil, chopped fresh or canned tomatoes and minced garlic.

> 1 **tablespoon whole white or black peppercorns**
> ¾ **teaspoon dried thyme leaves**
> 1 **small bay leaf (about 1 inch), broken in small pieces**
> 4 **boned and skinned chicken-breast halves (about 4 ounces each), flattened (see Flattening Chicken Breasts, page 23)**
> ¼ **teaspoon salt**
> 3 **tablespoons minced shallots or white part of green onions**
> 6 **medium-size cloves garlic, peeled and halved lengthwise (optional)**
> 1 **tablespoon butter or margarine**
> 1 **tablespoon chopped fresh parsley**
> ⅓ **cup dry white wine (see Note)**
> **For garnish: fresh parsley sprigs**

1. In a blender or a food processor, process peppercorns, thyme and bay-leaf pieces until bay leaf is no longer visible and peppercorns are coarsely cracked.

2. Sprinkle chicken with salt, the pepper mixture, shallots and garlic, if using, pressing lightly onto surface so that seasonings cling. Cover with a sheet of waxed paper and let stand at room temperature for 2 hours. Discard garlic.

3. Heat butter in a large nonstick skillet over medium heat until it foams. Add chicken and cook about 2 minutes per side, until golden brown on the outside and the pink color is almost gone in the center. Remove to a heated platter and sprinkle with chopped parsley.

4. Add wine to skillet and raise heat to high. Boil about 2 minutes, stirring often, until liquid is reduced to 3 tablespoons. Spoon sauce over chicken breasts and garnish with parsley sprigs.

Makes 4 servings. Per serving: 145 calories, 22 grams protein, 1 gram carbohydrate, 5 grams fat, 65 milligrams cholesterol with butter, 56 milligrams cholesterol with margarine, 213 milligrams sodium

Note: Wine may be omitted. Instead, add 1 additional tablespoon butter to skillet, stirring to mix with juices. Spoon over chicken and garnish.

Every Part
of the Chicken

Chicken comes conveniently packaged these days to suit your recipe and your family's preference. Any of the following recipes that call for a whole chicken can be adapted to use cut-up chickens or particular chicken parts. Adjust cooking time if needed. Chicken is done when the meat is firm but tender and no longer pink in the center or near the bone. Keep a close eye out while cooking—dry chicken is nobody's favorite.

🕐 **MAKE-AHEAD**
♥ **LOW-CALORIE**
Chili Chicken

This is excellent when freshly made; it can also be refrigerated for up to two days and reheated. Good go-withs are buttered corn kernels or corn bread and a green salad.

      8 **chicken drumsticks (about 2 pounds), skinned**
    ½ **teaspoon salt**
    ¼ **teaspoon pepper**
   2½ **tablespoons olive oil**
      2 **cups finely chopped onions (2 large)**
      1 **can (14 ½ ounces) tomatoes, undrained**
      4 **teaspoons chili powder**
      2 **teaspoons minced fresh garlic**
      1 **teaspoon dried oregano leaves**
    ½ **teaspoon ground cumin**
    ¼ **teaspoon granulated sugar**
      2 **teaspoons finely grated unsweetened chocolate (optional)**
For garnish: fresh cilantro leaves

1. Season chicken with salt and pepper.

2. Heat 2 tablespoons of the oil in a large, deep, heavy skillet. Add drumsticks, 4 at a time, and cook over medium heat about 10 minutes, turning occasionally, until lightly browned. Remove with a slotted spoon to a bowl.

3. Drain off all but 2 tablespoons pan drippings, or, if necessary, add more oil to measure 2 tablespoons.

4. Add onions and cook about 10 minutes, stirring occasionally, until light golden.

5. Add remaining ingredients except chocolate and cilantro, stirring to break up tomatoes. Bring to a boil over medium-high heat.

6. Add chicken and spoon sauce over top. Reduce heat to medium-low. Cover and simmer 20 to 25 minutes, stirring sauce and turning drumsticks occasionally, until just tender.

7. Stir in chocolate, if desired, until blended. Remove from heat. Sprinkle with cilantro leaves just before serving.

Makes 4 servings. Per serving (without chocolate): 282 calories, 28 grams protein, 13 grams carbohydrate, 13 grams fat, 94 milligrams cholesterol, 576 milligrams sodium

Chili Chicken

Pan-Fried Chicken with Milk Gravy

1 large egg
2 cups plus 1 tablespoon milk
1 broiler-fryer chicken (2½ to 3 pounds), cut up
1 cup vegetable oil for frying
¾ cup all-purpose flour
1 teaspoon paprika
1½ teaspoons salt

1. Beat egg and 1 tablespoon of the milk in a medium-size bowl until blended. Add chicken pieces and turn to coat.

2. Heat oil in a large, deep, heavy skillet over medium-high heat.

3. Meanwhile, mix ½ cup of the flour and the paprika in a large plastic food bag. Add 2 to 3 chicken pieces at a time. Close bag and shake until chicken is coated. Shake off excess flour mixture.

4. Carefully place chicken skin-side down in the skillet. Increase heat to high and fry, turning once with tongs, 1½ minutes per side, until golden brown.

5. Cover; reduce heat to medium and fry 8 to 10 minutes per side, until chicken is no longer pink near the bone.

6. Uncover skillet and increase heat to high. Fry chicken 1 to 2 minutes longer, until crisp. Drain on paper towels.

7. Season chicken with ½ teaspoon of the salt and transfer to a heated serving platter.

8. Pour off all but 2 tablespoons pan drippings. Add remaining ¼ cup flour and 1 teaspoon salt to skillet, stirring to scrape up browned bits on bottom. Cook over medium-low heat 2 to 3 minutes, stirring constantly, until smooth and frothy.

9. Gradually whisk in remaining 2 cups milk. Increase heat to medium and whisk until gravy is smooth and thickened. Serve with chicken.

Makes 4 servings. Per serving: 569 calories, 52 grams protein, 26 grams carbohydrate, 27 grams fat, 276 milligrams cholesterol, 743 milligrams sodium

---

★ **SPECIAL—AND WORTH IT**
Chicken Country-Style

Refrigerate fresh herbs in a jar with the stems standing in 2 inches of water. Cover leaves with a plastic bag. Herbs will stay fresh up to a week. (Change water every couple of days.)

2 tablespoons olive oil
1 broiler-fryer chicken (about 3½ pounds), cut up
1 cup diced carrots
¾ cup thinly sliced celery
¾ cup chopped onion
½ cup chopped green bell pepper
2 cups coarsely chopped peeled fresh tomatoes
½ cup dry white wine
2 teaspoons minced fresh oregano leaves
2 teaspoons minced fresh rosemary leaves
1 teaspoon salt
¼ teaspoon pepper
Herb Seasoning
½ cup minced fresh parsley
1 tablespoon grated fresh lemon peel
1½ teaspoons minced fresh garlic

1. Heat oil in a large heavy skillet over medium heat. Add chicken and brown on all sides. Remove to a plate.

2. Add carrots, celery, onion and bell pepper to skillet. Cook, stirring to scrape up browned bits, until onion is tender and vegetables are lightly coated with oil.

3. Add tomatoes, wine, oregano, rosemary, salt and pepper to skillet and mix gently. Remove vegetables with a slotted spoon to a bowl.

4. Return chicken to skillet skin-side up. Pour into skillet any juices that have collected on plate. Spoon vegetables over chicken.

5. Bring to a boil over medium-high heat. Cover; reduce heat to low and simmer 25 to 35 minutes, basting twice with pan juices, until chicken is fork-tender. Meanwhile, mix all Herb Seasoning ingredients in a small bowl. Cover and set aside.

6. Transfer chicken and vegetables to a heated platter with a slotted spoon.

7. Boil juices over high heat 3 to 5 minutes, until slightly thickened and reduced by half.

8. Reduce heat to medium and stir in Herb Seasoning. Simmer 3 minutes, spoon over chicken and serve.

Makes 6 servings. Per serving: 408 calories, 42 grams protein, 11 grams carbohydrate, 20 grams fat, 215 milligrams cholesterol, 485 milligrams sodium

Curried Chicken and Corn

Serve with steamed white or brown rice and pass mango chutney at the table.

> 1 tablespoon vegetable oil
> 1¼ cups chopped onions
> 2 teaspoons curry powder, or to taste
> 1¼ pounds boned and skinned chicken-breast halves, trimmed of fat, cut in 1-inch chunks
> 1 package (10 ounces) frozen corn kernels, thawed
> ¾ cup plain nonfat yogurt, stirred with 1 tablespoon all-purpose flour

For garnish: chopped fresh parsley

1. Heat oil in a large heavy skillet over medium heat. Add onions and stir in curry powder. Cook about 3 minutes, stirring two or three times, until onions are nearly tender.

2. Add chicken. Stir-fry 5 to 7 minutes, until chicken is no longer pink.

3. Stir corn into skillet. When corn is hot, reduce heat to low. Stir in yogurt mixture and simmer about 2 minutes, until sauce is smooth. Transfer to a heated platter, sprinkle with parsley and serve.

Makes 4 servings. Per serving: 299 calories, 40 grams protein, 23 grams carbohydrate, 6 grams fat, 84 milligrams cholesterol, 133 milligrams sodium

Curried Chicken and Corn

Georgia Peach and Chicken Skillet

To peel peaches, dip them in a saucepan of boiling water for about 30 seconds (longer for hard peaches). Lift them from the water with a slotted spoon and cool under cold running water, then slip off skins.

> 1 teaspoon salt
> ½ teaspoon ground ginger
> ¼ teaspoon paprika
> 1 broiler-fryer chicken (2½ to 3 pounds), cut up
> 2 tablespoons vegetable oil
> 1 cup chicken broth
> 3 large ripe peaches (about 1¼ pounds), peeled and pitted
> 2 tablespoons packed light-brown sugar
> 2 teaspoons cornstarch, stirred with 2 tablespoons water

1. Mix salt, ginger and paprika and sprinkle over chicken.

2. Heat oil in a large skillet over medium heat. Add chicken and brown on all sides. Carefully pour off and discard drippings.

3. Add broth to skillet and bring to a simmer. Reduce heat to low; cover and simmer 30 minutes, until chicken is fork-tender. Remove chicken to a heated platter and keep warm.

4. Meanwhile, mash 1 peach in a bowl with a fork to make ½ cup puree. Cut remaining peaches into eighths.

5. Stir brown sugar, peach puree and cornstarch mixture into skillet. Bring to a boil over medium-high heat. Reduce heat and simmer 1 minute, stirring constantly, until thickened. Add peach slices and toss gently until hot. Spoon sauce and peaches over chicken and serve.

Makes 4 servings. Per serving: 422 calories, 44 grams protein, 18 grams carbohydrate, 18 grams fat, 199 milligrams cholesterol, 717 milligrams sodium

Chicken-Vegetable Skillet with Rice

If you can't find boned chicken thighs in your market, you can substitute boneless chicken or turkey breasts. Serve orange wedges or clementines and crisp wafer cookies for dessert.

1⅓ cups water
½ teaspoon salt
1⅓ cups 5-minute rice
1 tablespoon vegetable oil
1½ pounds boned and skinned chicken thighs, cut in narrow strips
1 tablespoon minced fresh garlic
1 bag (16 ounces) frozen mixed Oriental vegetables (green beans, broccoli, onion and mushrooms)
1½ tablespoons cornstarch
1½ teaspoons ground ginger
3 tablespoons soy sauce
¾ cup chicken broth (see Note)
½ cup unsalted dry-roasted peanuts

1. Bring water and salt to a boil in a medium-size saucepan. Stir in rice; cover, remove from heat and set aside.

2. Heat oil in a large heavy skillet or wok over medium-high heat. Add chicken and garlic and cook about 3 minutes, stirring frequently, until chicken is lightly browned.

3. Add vegetables and cook about 2 minutes, stirring often, until thawed.

4. Meanwhile, mix cornstarch, ginger, soy sauce and broth in a bowl until blended. Pour into skillet and stir until sauce boils and thickens.

5. Reduce heat to low. Cover and simmer 2 minutes, until chicken is no longer pink in the center. Stir in peanuts. Serve over the rice.

Makes 4 servings. Per serving: 607 calories, 57 grams protein, 40 grams carbohydrate, 23 grams fat, 158 milligrams cholesterol, 1,499 milligrams sodium

Note: If making chicken broth from a bouillon cube and hot water, cool to room temperature or chill before mixing with cornstarch.

♥ LOW-CALORIE
Skillet Cacciatore

You can serve this in less than 25 minutes—on its own or ladled over steaming pasta.

12 ounces boned and skinned chicken thighs, cut in 1½-inch cubes (about 2 cups)
3 tablespoons olive oil
2 tablespoons dry white wine or 1 tablespoon lemon juice
1 teaspoon minced fresh garlic
1 teaspoon chopped fresh rosemary leaves or ½ teaspoon dried rosemary, crumbled
½ teaspoon salt
¼ teaspoon crushed red-pepper flakes
6 ounces small mushrooms, halved (about 2 cups)
1 medium-size carrot, cut diagonally in thin slices (about ½ cup)
1 box (10 ounces) frozen whole petite green beans, thawed
½ cup frozen small white onions, thawed
1 can (16 ounces) sliced stewed tomatoes
1 tablespoon tomato paste

1. Put chicken in a medium-size bowl and mix with 1 tablespoon of the oil, the wine, garlic, rosemary, salt and crushed red pepper.

2. Place a large, deep skillet over high heat about 3 minutes, until very hot. Add 1 tablespoon of the oil; tilt pan to coat bottom. Add chicken mixture and stir-fry 1½ to 2 minutes, until chicken is no longer pink. Transfer to a large bowl.

3. Heat remaining 1 tablespoon oil in skillet. Add mushrooms and carrot and stir-fry 2 minutes. Add green beans and onions and stir-fry 1 to 1½ minutes, until vegetables are crisp-tender. Add to bowl with chicken.

4. Put stewed tomatoes and tomato paste in skillet and stir to blend. Bring to a boil; boil 1 minute, until slightly thickened.

5. Return chicken and vegetables to skillet. Stir 1 minute, until blended and hot. Serve alone or over pasta.

Makes 4 servings. Per serving: 283 calories, 24 grams protein, 15 grams carbohydrate, 15 grams fat, 64 milligrams cholesterol, 492 milligrams sodium

Starting with Cooked

These recipes offer inventive ways to make use of leftovers or "planned-overs." If your leftover chicken has disappeared, you can substitute canned or the cooked chicken now sold packaged at meat counters.

♥ **LOW-CALORIE**

Stir-fried Chicken with Green Beans and Cashews

This recipe can also be made with leftover turkey.

3 tablespoons water
2 tablespoons soy sauce
2 tablespoons cornstarch
1 teaspoon granulated sugar
1 teaspoon cider vinegar
1 teaspoon Oriental sesame oil
1 tablespoon vegetable oil
1 cup frozen chopped green bell peppers and onions
1 package (8 ounces) frozen petite green beans or sugar-snap peas
2 cups diced cooked chicken (10 ounces)
⅓ cup salted cashews or salted peanuts

1. Mix water, soy sauce, cornstarch, sugar, vinegar and sesame oil in a small bowl until blended.

2. Heat vegetable oil in a large heavy skillet or wok over medium-high heat. Add bell peppers and onions and green beans. Stir-fry 4 to 5 minutes, until vegetables are crisp-tender.

3. Stir in chicken, nuts and soy-sauce mixture and bring to a boil. Boil 1 minute, stirring constantly, until sauce thickens. Serve immediately.

Makes 4 servings. Per serving (with green beans and cashews): 277 calories, 27 grams protein, 14 grams carbohydrate, 13 grams fat, 56 milligrams cholesterol, 759 milligrams sodium

Spicy Orange Chicken

Spicy Orange Chicken

Delicious over hot cooked rice. Add a watercress-and-cucumber salad to complete the meal.

¼ cup vegetable oil
½ cup sliced green onions
1 teaspoon minced fresh garlic
1½ cups orange juice, preferably fresh-squeezed
¼ cup Zante currants or raisins
1 tablespoon packed brown sugar
1 tablespoon Worcestershire sauce
¼ to ½ teaspoon crushed red-pepper flakes or hot-pepper sauce
4 teaspoons cornstarch, stirred with 4 teaspoons water
2 cans (5 ounces each) chunk white chicken, drained, or 1⅓ cups diced cooked chicken (about 8 ounces)

1. Heat oil in a medium-size skillet over medium heat. Stir in onions and garlic. Cook 1 to 2 minutes, stirring often, until tender.

2. Stir in orange juice, currants, sugar, Worcestershire sauce and crushed red pepper. Bring to a boil and simmer 5 minutes.

3. Stir cornstarch mixture again, then stir into skillet. Bring to a boil. Simmer 1 minute, stirring constantly, until thickened.

4. Add chicken to skillet, stir gently and simmer until hot. Serve alone or over rice.

Makes 4 servings. Per serving: 329 calories, 16 grams protein, 27 grams carbohydrate, 18 grams fat, 60 milligrams cholesterol, 291 milligrams sodium

Sicilian Chicken

½ teaspoon minced fresh garlic
1 tablespoon olive oil
2 cans (about 16 ounces each)
    tomatoes, undrained, broken up
2 cans (6¾ ounces each) chunk white
    chicken, undrained
1 package (9 ounces) frozen Italian
    green beans
¾ cup pitted ripe olives
2 teaspoons dried basil leaves
2 cups medium egg noodles

1. Cook garlic in oil in a large skillet over medium-high heat 1 minute, until golden.

2. Add remaining ingredients in order given. Stir gently until noodles are covered with liquid.

3. Bring to a boil. Reduce heat to low; cover and simmer 8 to 10 minutes, stirring occasionally, until noodles are tender. Transfer to a heated dish and serve.

Makes 4 servings. Per serving: 368 calories, 26 grams protein, 28 grams carbohydrate, 17 grams fat, 89 milligrams cholesterol, 859 milligrams sodium

Indonesian Chicken Curry

2 tablespoons butter or margarine
1 large apple, peeled, halved, cored
    and sliced
¼ cup chopped onion
1 teaspoon minced fresh garlic
2 tablespoons all-purpose flour
2 teaspoons curry powder
2 teaspoons instant chicken-broth
    granules
1¼ cups milk
2 cups cubed cooked chicken or
    turkey
1 jar (4.5 ounces) mushrooms,
    drained
8 ounces egg noodles, freshly cooked
    and drained

1. Melt butter in a large skillet over medium heat. Add apple, onion and garlic and cook 4 minutes, stirring occasionally, until tender.

2. Stir in flour, curry powder and broth granules. Slowly stir in milk. Add chicken and mushrooms.

3. Bring to a boil. Reduce heat to low and simmer 10 minutes, stirring occasionally, until hot. Serve over the noodles.

Makes 4 servings. Per serving: 505 calories, 33 grams protein, 56 grams carbohydrate, 16 grams fat, 145 milligrams cholesterol with butter, 127 milligrams cholesterol with margarine, 544 milligrams sodium

Sicilian Chicken

Chicken Livers

Don't overcook chicken livers, or they'll be tough and bitter. They're most tender when still slightly pink in the center.

Creamy Chicken-Liver Skillet

Yogurt, instead of high-fat sour cream, makes this sauce rich.

- **12 ounces chicken livers, halved and trimmed**
- **¼ cup all-purpose flour**
- **4 tablespoons butter or margarine**
- **1½ cups thinly sliced onions**
- **1 teaspoon paprika**
- **½ teaspoon salt**
- **Pepper to taste**
- **1 cup plain low-fat yogurt**

1. Coat livers in flour.

2. Heat 3 tablespoons of the butter in a large skillet over high heat until it foams. Add livers and cook until browned, turning frequently. Remove with a slotted spoon to a bowl.

3. Melt remaining 1 tablespoon butter in skillet. Add onions, reduce heat to medium and cook until tender, stirring occasionally.

4. Return livers to skillet. Season with paprika, salt and pepper. Cover and cook about 5 minutes, until livers are barely pink inside. Add yogurt and stir just until hot. (Do not let mixture boil.) Transfer to a heated platter and serve.

Makes 4 servings. Per serving: 323 calories, 26 grams protein, 17 grams carbohydrate, 16 grams fat, 675 milligrams cholesterol with butter, 639 milligrams cholesterol with margarine, 494 milligrams sodium

Stir-fried Chicken Livers

The best chicken livers are light-colored and firm. If the livers are very wet, put them in a sieve and shake off the liquid before stir-frying.

- **1⅓ cups water**
- **½ teaspoon salt**
- **1⅓ cups 5-minute rice**
- **1 pound chicken livers, halved and trimmed**
- **¼ cup all-purpose flour**
- **2 tablespoons vegetable oil**
- **1 can (8 ounces) sliced water chestnuts, drained**
- **4 medium-size green onions, cut diagonally in 1-inch pieces**
- **¾ cup chicken broth**
- **1 tablespoon soy sauce**
- **½ teaspoon Oriental sesame oil**
- **1 cup cherry tomatoes, cut in halves**

1. Bring water and salt to a boil in a medium-size saucepan over high heat. Stir in rice; cover, remove from heat and set aside.

2. Coat livers in flour in a plastic food bag.

3. Heat oil in a large skillet over high heat. Add livers, water chestnuts and green onions and stir-fry 5 minutes, until livers are browned outside and slightly pink inside. Remove to a plate.

4. Add broth, soy sauce and sesame oil to skillet. Reduce heat to low and simmer 2 minutes, until slightly thickened.

5. Return liver mixture to skillet and add cherry tomatoes. Simmer until hot. Serve with the rice.

Makes 4 servings. Per serving: 447 calories, 36 grams protein, 47 grams carbohydrate, 12 grams fat, 849 milligrams cholesterol, 810 milligrams sodium

Quick Chicken-Liver Sauté

- **¼ cup all-purpose flour**
- **½ teaspoon salt**
- **1 pound chicken livers, halved and trimmed**
- **3 tablespoons butter or margarine**
- **1 medium-size onion, chopped**
- **2 tablespoons dry sherry or chicken broth**
- **For garnish: chopped fresh parsley**

1. Mix flour and salt in a plastic food bag. Add livers and toss to coat.

2. Melt butter in a large skillet over medium heat. Add onion and cook 2 minutes, stirring often.

3. Push onion to sides of skillet. Raise heat to medium-high. Add livers and cook 5 minutes, turning once, until browned.

4. Add sherry, stirring to scrape up browned bits. Reduce heat to low; cover and cook 2 minutes, until livers are tender. Transfer to a heated platter, sprinkle with parsley and serve.

Makes 4 servings. Per serving: 300 calories, 31 grams protein, 11 grams carbohydrate, 14 grams fat, 873 milligrams cholesterol with butter, 846 milligrams cholesterol with margarine, 443 milligrams sodium

Chicken Livers in Basil-Tomato Sauce

If you can't find Italian green beans, substitute green snap beans.

⅓ cup butter or margarine
1 pound chicken livers, halved and trimmed
½ teaspoon salt
½ teaspoon pepper
⅔ cup minced green onions
4 ounces thinly sliced mushrooms (about 1½ cups)
⅓ cup dry white wine
2 large fresh tomatoes, peeled, seeded and finely chopped, or 2 canned whole tomatoes, seeded and finely chopped
¼ teaspoon granulated sugar
6 tablespoons minced fresh basil leaves or ¾ teaspoon crumbled dried basil
½ teaspoon minced fresh rosemary leaves or dried rosemary
1½ teaspoons minced fresh garlic
1 cup heavy cream
1¼ pounds Italian green beans, trimmed, cut in 2-inch lengths (about 5 cups)
3 tablespoons chopped fresh parsley

1. Heat butter in a large heavy skillet over medium heat until it bubbles and starts to brown. Add livers and cook 5 minutes, turning occasionally, until browned. Remove from skillet with a slotted spoon and season with salt and pepper.

2. Add green onions and mushrooms to skillet and cook about 3 minutes, until tender.

3. Add wine; increase heat to high, stirring to loosen browned bits. Simmer about 3 minutes, until wine is completely evaporated.

4. Return livers to skillet. Stir in tomatoes, sugar, basil, rosemary, garlic and cream. Simmer about 5 minutes, until slightly thickened.

5. Meanwhile, cook beans in boiling salted water about 7 minutes, until crisp-tender. Drain well.

6. Arrange beans on heated dinner plates. Spoon liver mixture over top. Sprinkle with parsley and serve.

Makes 4 generous servings. Per serving: 626 calories, 36 grams protein, 23 grams carbohydrate, 43 grams fat, 972 milligrams cholesterol with butter, 927 milligrams cholesterol with margarine, 557 milligrams sodium

Chicken Livers, Peppers and Rice

1⅓ cups water
1 chicken-bouillon cube or 1 teaspoon instant broth granules
1⅓ cups 5-minute rice
¼ teaspoon Italian dried-herb seasoning
3 tablespoons olive oil
1 large red onion (about 8 ounces), thinly sliced
1 teaspoon minced fresh garlic
1 pound chicken livers, halved and trimmed
1 jar (7 ounces) roasted red peppers, drained (tear large pieces in half)
½ teaspoon salt
¼ teaspoon pepper

1. Bring water and bouillon to a boil in a small saucepan over high heat, stirring to dissolve bouillon. Stir in rice and Italian seasoning. Remove from heat, cover and set aside.

2. Heat oil in a large nonstick skillet over high heat. Add onion and garlic and cook 3 to 4 minutes, stirring often, until onion starts to brown.

3. Add livers and cook 5 to 6 minutes, turning them as they brown, until just barely pink in the center.

4. Stir in red peppers, salt and pepper and cook 1 minute, until peppers are heated through. Serve over the rice.

Makes 4 servings. Per serving: 427 calories, 33 grams protein, 34 grams carbohydrate, 15 grams fat, 847 milligrams cholesterol, 580 milligrams sodium

Chicken Livers, Peppers and Rice

Turkey Cutlets

An excellent way to cook thinly sliced turkey breast cutlets quickly is frying. If you use just a little oil and a nonstick skillet, you will get a browned exterior for relatively few calories. There is really no test for doneness, other than your eye. As soon as they're browned, they're done.

★ **SPECIAL—AND WORTH IT**
♥ **LOW-CALORIE**

Turkey Scaloppine with Asparagus, Chives and Mustard Cream Sauce

Serve with egg noodles or mashed potatoes to soak up the sauce.

¼ **cup all-purpose flour**
Pepper to taste
4 **thin-sliced turkey-breast cutlets (about 4 ounces each)**
3 **tablespoons vegetable oil**
1 **cup chicken broth**
½ **cup sour cream**
1 **teaspoon Dijon mustard, or to taste**
1 **package (10 ounces) frozen asparagus spears, thawed and cut in ½-inch pieces**
2 **tablespoons snipped fresh or frozen chives**
For garnish: lemon slices, parsley sprigs

1. Mix flour and pepper on a sheet of waxed paper. Coat cutlets in seasoned flour.

2. Heat oil in a large nonstick skillet over medium-high heat. Add cutlets without crowding. Cook 3 minutes per side, until golden brown and tender. Remove to a heated platter.

3. Drain oil from skillet. Pour in broth and bring to a boil. Boil about 3 minutes, until reduced to ½ cup.

4. Reduce heat under skillet to medium-low. Stir sour cream and mustard into skillet. Add asparagus and chives and simmer until sauce is the consistency of heavy cream. Spoon over cutlets; garnish with lemon slices and parsley and serve.

Makes 4 servings. Per serving: 279 calories, 38 grams protein, 8 grams carbohydrate, 10 grams fat, 95 milligrams cholesterol, 298 milligrams sodium

Turkey Scaloppine with Asparagus, Chives and Mustard Cream Sauce

Turkey Scaloppine with Mushrooms

Serve with *risi e bisi*, which is Italian for "rice and peas." Cook rice in chicken broth until tender. Remove from heat. Stir in frozen peas, cover and let stand 5 minutes to heat peas.

2½ **tablespoons all-purpose flour**
¾ **teaspoon salt**
¼ **teaspoon pepper**
8 **thin-sliced turkey-breast cutlets (about 4 ounces each; cut larger turkey cutlets in half)**
3 **tablespoons butter or margarine**
2 **tablespoons vegetable oil**
3 **tablespoons red-wine vinegar**
1 **can (3 ounces) sliced broiled-in-butter mushrooms, drained, liquid reserved**
2 **tablespoons chopped fresh parsley**

1. Mix flour, salt and pepper on a sheet of waxed paper. Coat cutlets in flour mixture.

2. Put a heat-proof platter in oven. Set oven to 200°F.

3. Heat 2 tablespoons of the butter and the oil in a large skillet (not cast-iron) over medium heat until butter melts. Add half the cutlets and cook 2 to 3 minutes per side, just until lightly browned.

4. Transfer to platter in oven, leaving door slightly ajar. Repeat with remaining cutlets.

5. Add vinegar and juice from mushrooms to skillet. Stir to scrape up browned bits from bottom.

6. When liquid is bubbling, stir in remaining 1 tablespoon butter and the mushrooms. Continue to boil 1 to 2 minutes, stirring constantly, until liquid is slightly reduced and shiny. Stir in parsley. Spoon sauce over cutlets and serve.

Makes 4 servings. Per serving: 326 calories, 28 grams protein, 6 grams carbohydrate, 21 grams fat, 103 milligrams cholesterol with butter, 76 milligrams cholesterol with margarine, 716 milligrams sodium

Turkey with Corn and Spinach

A good accompaniment to this dish is sliced ripe tomatoes drizzled with Italian dressing.

¼ **cup all-purpose flour**
1½ **teaspoons salt**
⅛ **teaspoon pepper**
1¼ **pounds thin-sliced turkey-breast cutlets**
2 **tablespoons vegetable oil**
1 **teaspoon minced fresh garlic**
¾ **cup chicken broth**
1 **package (16 ounces) frozen corn kernels (3½ cups)**
1 **bag (10 ounces) fresh spinach, rinsed and tough stems removed**

1. Mix flour, salt and pepper on a sheet of waxed paper. Coat cutlets in flour mixture.

2. Heat oil in a large skillet over medium-high heat. Add half the cutlets and cook 2 minutes per side, until golden brown. Remove to a plate. Repeat with remaining cutlets.

3. Add garlic to skillet and cook 1 minute, stirring constantly. Add chicken broth and stir to scrape up browned bits from bottom of skillet.

4. Stir in corn and top with half the spinach. Cover and simmer 1 minute, until spinach wilts. Add remaining spinach. Cover and cook 1 minute longer, until spinach is wilted. Stir to mix with corn.

5. Return browned cutlets to skillet. Spoon some of the corn and spinach over cutlets. Cover skillet and cook 1 minute, until turkey is hot. Transfer to a heated platter and serve.

Makes 4 servings. Per serving: 366 calories, 25 grams protein, 32 grams carbohydrate, 18 grams fat, 70 milligrams cholesterol, 943 milligrams sodium

Turkey with Corn and Spinach

Turkey Saltimbocca with Escarole

♥ **LOW-CALORIE**

Turkey Saltimbocca with Escarole

A dish that's *saltimbocca* (literally "jump-in-the-mouth") contains ham and sage. If you prefer to use fresh sage rather than dried, place a leaf on each cutlet under the ham. This dish is good with crusty Italian bread. Serve fresh strawberries for dessert and small cups of espresso with lemon twists.

½ **teaspoon dried sage leaves**
½ **teaspoon pepper**
8 **thin-sliced turkey-breast cutlets (about 2 ounces each; cut larger turkey cutlets in half)**
4 **slices fully cooked ham (1 ounce each), each cut in half**
1 **tablespoon butter or margarine**
½ **teaspoon minced fresh garlic**
1 **medium-size head escarole (about 12 ounces), rinsed and torn in bite-size pieces**
1 **can (8½ ounces) tomatoes, drained and chopped**
¼ **teaspoon salt**

1. Sprinkle sage and pepper on one side of each cutlet. Top each cutlet with a half slice of ham.

2. Melt butter in a large skillet over medium-high heat. Add cutlets ham-side down and cook about 1½ minutes, until browned. Turn with a wide spatula and cook 1½ minutes longer, until browned. Remove to a heated platter and cover with foil to keep warm.

3. Add garlic, escarole, tomatoes and salt to skillet and reduce heat to medium. Stir about 2 minutes, until tomatoes are hot and escarole has wilted. Serve cutlets with the escarole, pouring juices from skillet over the meat.

Makes 4 servings. Per serving: 231 calories, 34 grams protein, 5 grams carbohydrate, 7 grams fat, 95 milligrams cholesterol with butter, 86 milligrams cholesterol with margarine, 777 milligrams sodium

Turkey Scaloppine in Lemon-Caper Sauce

To prevent the flour from becoming pasty and gummy, flour the turkey cutlets just before cooking. Serve the scaloppine with lemon slices and one-pot pasta-and-vegetables (add a package of frozen mixed vegetables to pasta 5 minutes before pasta cooking time is up).

1 **pound thin-sliced turkey-breast**
  cutlets
¼ **cup all-purpose flour**
2 **tablespoons olive oil**
½ **cup dry white wine**
2 **tablespoons lemon juice**
2 **tablespoons chopped fresh parsley**
2 **tablespoons drained capers**
½ **teaspoon Worcestershire sauce**
½ **teaspoon salt**
½ **teaspoon pepper**
For garnish: lemon slices

1. Lightly coat turkey cutlets in flour.

2. Heat 1 tablespoon of the oil in a large nonstick skillet over medium-high heat. Add half the cutlets and cook about 1 minute per side, until lightly browned. Remove cutlets to plate. Repeat with remaining 1 tablespoon oil and cutlets.

3. Add wine, lemon juice, parsley, capers, Worcestershire sauce, salt and pepper to skillet. Raise heat to high and bring to a boil. Boil 1 to 2 minutes, stirring to scrape up browned bits on bottom of skillet, until sauce is slightly thickened.

4. Return cutlets to skillet and spoon sauce over them. Transfer to plates, garnish with lemon slices and serve.

Makes 4 servings. Per serving: 222 calories, 28 grams protein, 7 grams carbohydrate, 9 grams fat, 70 milligrams cholesterol, 470 milligrams sodium

Turkey Scaloppine in Lemon-Caper Sauce

Turkey Scallops à L'Orange

Serve with Sesame Asparagus (recipe follows).

- 2 tablespoons butter or margarine
- ½ teaspoon minced fresh garlic
- 1¼ pounds thin-sliced turkey-breast cutlets
- ½ cup orange juice
- 1 teaspoon lemon juice
- 2 teaspoons cornstarch
- ½ teaspoon salt

Pepper to taste

1. Melt butter with garlic in a large nonstick skillet over medium heat until butter foams.

2. Add turkey cutlets and cook 1 to 2 minutes per side until lightly browned. Remove to a heated platter, cover loosely and keep warm.

3. Stir orange juice, lemon juice, cornstarch, salt and pepper in a small bowl until smooth.

4. Stir mixture into skillet, scraping up browned bits on bottom. Boil 1 minute, stirring constantly, until thickened. Pour over cutlets and serve.

Makes 4 servings. Per serving: 322 calories, 47 grams protein, 5 grams carbohydrate, 11 grams fat, 127 milligrams cholesterol with butter, 109 milligrams cholesterol with margarine, 453 milligrams sodium

Sesame Asparagus

Quick steaming ensures bright-green asparagus.

- 2 tablespoons sesame seed
- 1 tablespoon butter or margarine
- 1 tablespoon vegetable oil
- ¼ cup water or chicken broth
- 2 pounds fresh asparagus, tough ends trimmed, cut in 2-inch pieces
- ¼ teaspoon salt

Pepper to taste

1. Cook sesame seed in butter and oil in a large skillet over medium heat until lightly toasted.

2. Add water and asparagus and bring to a boil.

3. Cover and simmer about 4 minutes, until asparagus is crisp-tender.

4. Season with salt and pepper. Transfer to a heated dish and serve.

Makes 4 servings. Per serving (with water): 123 calories, 5 grams protein, 9 grams carbohydrate, 9 grams fat, 9 milligrams cholesterol with butter, 0 milligrams cholesterol with margarine, 174 milligrams sodium

★ SPECIAL—AND WORTH IT

Turkey Scallops with Tarragon Sauce

- ⅓ cup packaged dry bread crumbs
- ¾ teaspoon salt
- ½ teaspoon dried tarragon leaves, crumbled
- 1¼ pounds thin-sliced turkey-breast cutlets
- 3 tablespoons butter or margarine
- 3 tablespoons olive oil
- ½ cup dry white wine
- ½ cup heavy cream
- ¼ cup crumbled feta cheese (optional)

1. Mix bread crumbs, salt and tarragon in a shallow pan or pie plate.

2. Coat turkey cutlets in crumbs, pressing crumbs firmly onto surface.

3. Heat butter and oil in a large heavy skillet over medium heat until butter melts. Add cutlets and cook about 3 minutes per side, until golden brown and crisp. Remove to a heated platter and keep warm.

4. Add wine and cream to skillet. Cook over high heat about 3 minutes, stirring constantly, until slightly thickened. Stir in feta cheese, if desired, and heat through. Pour sauce over cutlets and serve.

Makes 4 servings. Per serving (with feta cheese): 580 calories, 49 grams protein, 8 grams carbohydrate, 37 grams fat, 182 milligrams cholesterol with butter, 155 milligrams cholesterol with margarine, 770 milligrams sodium

Turkey Schnitzel Dijon

🕐 **MAKE-AHEAD**

Turkey Schnitzel Dijon

Crisp turkey cutlets prepared and cooked like their veal counterparts are just as delicious and much less expensive. You can bread and refrigerate them a day ahead. They make an elegant meal with whole green beans, cooked crisptender and "straw" potatoes (see Note).

Whites from 2 large eggs
2 tablespoons water
2 tablespoons Dijon mustard
¼ teaspoon salt
¼ teaspoon pepper
1 pound thin-sliced turkey-breast cutlets
1 cup packaged seasoned dry bread crumbs
3 tablespoons olive oil
For garnish: fresh parsley sprigs and lemon slices

1. Mix egg whites, water, mustard, salt and pepper in a shallow dish with a fork until blended.

2. Dip turkey cutlets in egg-white mixture, then in crumbs to coat, gently pressing crumbs onto surface so that they adhere.

3. Heat 1½ tablespoons of the oil in a large nonstick skillet over medium-high heat. Add half the turkey cutlets and cook 1 minute per side, until lightly browned. Remove to a heated platter and keep warm.

4. Repeat with remaining 1½ tablespoons oil and cutlets.

5. Arrange on plates and garnish with parsley sprigs and lemon slices to squeeze over servings.

Makes 4 servings. Per serving: 343 calories, 32 grams protein, 22 grams carbohydrate, 13 grams fat, 72 milligrams cholesterol, 1,258 milligrams sodium

Note: To make "straw" potatoes, thaw frozen hashbrown patties. Crumble and deep-fry in hot oil just until golden brown and crisp. Drain potatoes on paper towels before serving.

Turkey-Vegetable Stir-fry

1⅓ cups water
½ teaspoon salt
1⅓ cups 5-minute rice
 1 tablespoon cornstarch
 5 teaspoons reduced-sodium
    soy sauce
 1 tablespoon Oriental sesame oil
 ¾ cup chicken broth (see Note)
 1 tablespoon vegetable oil
12 ounces thin-sliced turkey- or
    chicken-breast cutlets, cut
    crosswise in narrow strips (about
    2 cups)
 1 teaspoon minced fresh garlic
 1 bag (16 ounces) frozen mixed
    broccoli, red peppers, bamboo
    shoots and straw mushrooms
 1 cup 1-inch pieces diagonally sliced
    green onions

1. Bring water and salt to a boil in a medium-size saucepan over high heat. Stir in rice; remove from heat, cover and set aside.

2. Stir cornstarch, soy sauce, sesame oil and broth in a cup until blended.

3. Heat vegetable oil in a large, deep nonstick skillet or wok over high heat until hot but not smoking. Add turkey and garlic and stir-fry 1 minute, until turkey starts to brown.

4. Stir in vegetables and green onions. Cover and cook 3 to 4 minutes, stirring occasionally, until vegetables are hot and turkey is no longer pink in the center.

5. Stir cornstarch mixture again and pour into skillet. Bring to a boil, stirring constantly, until sauce is thickened and clear. Serve over the rice.

Makes 4 servings. Per serving: 279 calories, 22 grams protein, 34 grams carbohydrate, 5 grams fat, 43 milligrams cholesterol, 648 milligrams sodium

Note: If making broth with a bouillon cube and hot water, let broth cool before adding cornstarch.

Stir-fried Turkey with Melon

To trim snow-peas, snap off an end, pull the string that runs along one side and snap off the other end. For a special look, you can snip a V-shaped cut on the end of each snow-pea with kitchen shears.

---

 2 teaspoons soy sauce
 2 teaspoons rice-wine vinegar or
    cider vinegar
 1 teaspoon honey
 1 teaspoon cornstarch
 2 tablespoons vegetable oil
 1 teaspoon minced fresh garlic
 1 teaspoon grated fresh gingerroot or
    ½ teaspoon ground ginger
12 ounces thin-sliced turkey-breast
    cutlets, cut in 2-inch-wide strips
 1 large yellow or red bell pepper, cut
    in 1-inch chunks (about 1 cup)
 4 ounces snow-peas, trimmed
 2 cups 1-inch chunks cantaloupe or
    honeydew melon, or a
    combination

1. Stir soy sauce, vinegar, honey and cornstarch in a small bowl until smooth.

2. Heat oil in a large skillet or wok over high heat until hot but not smoking. Add garlic and gingerroot and cook about 30 seconds, stirring constantly, to flavor oil.

3. Add turkey and stir-fry 1 minute, until the pink color is almost gone.

4. Add bell pepper and snow-peas and stir-fry 2 to 3 minutes, until vegetables are crisp-tender.

5. Stir soy-sauce mixture again and add to skillet. Cook, stirring constantly, until sauce thickens.

6. Add melon and stir gently to mix. Remove from heat to dinner plates and serve.

Makes 4 servings. Per serving: 273 calories, 30 grams protein, 14 grams carbohydrate, 11 grams fat, 65 milligrams cholesterol, 306 milligrams sodium

Turkey Thighs

Turkey-Tomato Skillet with Melted Mozzarella

Choose any exotic mushroom for this dish, or use white button mushrooms. Smoked mozzarella cheese is available at most supermarket cheese counters and at Italian specialty stores.

> 3 tablespoons olive or vegetable oil
> 3 pounds turkey thighs, skinned, boned and cut in 1½-inch chunks
> 2 medium-size onions, coarsely chopped (about 1½ cups)
> 1 can (14 ½ ounces) tomatoes, undrained, broken up
> 1 teaspoon minced fresh garlic
> 1 teaspoon chopped fresh rosemary leaves or ½ teaspoon dried rosemary
> ½ teaspoon salt, or to taste
> ¼ teaspoon pepper, or to taste
> 4 ounces *each* yellow summer squash and zucchini, quartered lengthwise and cut in ½-inch-thick slices
> 1 can (6 ounces drained weight) pitted ripe olives, drained and sliced
> 4 ounces mushrooms, preferably oyster mushrooms, quartered
> 8 ounces smoked mozzarella cheese, sliced thin
> For garnish: fresh tomato wedges, fresh rosemary sprigs

1. Heat oil in a large skillet over medium-high heat. Add turkey and brown, stirring occasionally.

2. Reduce heat to medium-low. Add onions and cook 3 minutes, stirring often, until nearly tender.

3. Drain drippings from skillet. Stir in tomatoes, garlic, rosemary, salt and pepper and bring to a simmer.

4. Cover and simmer 45 minutes, stirring twice.

5. Stir in squashes, olives and mushrooms. Top with mozzarella slices. Cover and cook 10 to 15 minutes, until squashes are crisp-tender and cheese melts. Garnish with tomato wedges and rosemary sprigs. Serve from skillet.

Makes 6 servings. Per serving: 456 calories, 44 grams protein, 9 grams carbohydrate, 27 grams fat, 144 milligrams cholesterol, 610 milligrams sodium

Ground Turkey

Ground turkey is at least 50 percent lower in fat than other ground meats, which makes it a great choice if you're watching fat and calorie intake. Fresh ground turkey is now widely available.

♥ LOW-CALORIE
Plump Turkey Patties

Cabbage gives these patties a juicy sweetness. They're delicious with mashed potatoes and buttered baby carrots.

> 1 large egg
> ½ slice firm white bread, torn in small pieces
> 1 pound ground turkey
> 3 cups finely shredded green cabbage (10 ounces)
> 1 small onion, finely grated (⅓ cup)
> 1½ teaspoons ground coriander seed
> 1 teaspoon salt
> ¾ to 1 teaspoon pepper
> ¼ teaspoon ground nutmeg
> ¼ teaspoon granulated sugar
> 2 tablespoons butter or margarine

1. Beat egg in a large bowl. Stir in bread. Let soak 1 or 2 minutes, then whisk to break up bread.

2. Add turkey, cabbage, onion, coriander, salt, pepper, nutmeg and sugar. Mix until blended.

3. Shape into six 1-inch-thick patties.

4. Melt 1 tablespoon of the butter in a large skillet over medium heat. Add three patties. Cook about 6 minutes per side, until patties are browned and no longer pink in the center. Remove to a heated platter and keep warm. Repeat with remaining butter and patties. Serve.

Makes 6 servings. Per serving: 180 calories, 16 grams protein, 4 grams carbohydrate, 11 grams fat, 98 milligrams cholesterol with butter, 91 milligrams cholesterol with margarine, 428 milligrams sodium

Turkey-Tomato Skillet with Melted Mozzarella

Turkey Picadillo

Turkey Burgers with Gravy

1 pound ground turkey
1 cup herb-seasoned
    bread stuffing mix
½ cup sliced green onions
2 tablespoons mayonnaise
1 large egg
2 tablespoons vegetable oil
1 can (10 ounces) turkey gravy

1. Mix all ingredients except oil and gravy in a medium-size bowl until blended. Shape into four patties.

2. Heat oil in a large skillet over medium-high heat. Add patties and cook 4 to 5 minutes per side, until browned.

3. Pour gravy into skillet and reduce heat to medium-low. Cover and simmer 4 to 5 minutes, until gravy is hot and patties are no longer pink in the center. Transfer to plates and serve.

Makes 4 servings. Per serving: 448 calories, 24 grams protein, 14 grams carbohydrate, 32 grams fat, 169 milligrams cholesterol, 734 milligrams sodium

Turkey-Vegetable Stroganoff

8 ounces fine egg noodles
1 tablespoon vegetable oil
1 pound ground turkey
1 packet (¾ ounce) brown-gravy mix
2 cups frozen mixed vegetables
    (broccoli, cauliflower and carrots)
1 teaspoon Italian dried-herb
    seasoning
¾ teaspoon minced fresh garlic
½ teaspoon salt
¼ teaspoon pepper
¼ cup sour cream

1. Bring 8 cups water to a boil in a large covered saucepan over high heat. Add noodles and boil about 4 minutes, stirring often, until tender. Drain noodles in a colander. Rinse with hot water to prevent sticking and spread on a heated platter. Cover with foil to keep warm.

2. Meanwhile, heat oil in a large skillet over high heat. Crumble in turkey and cook 5 minutes, stirring often to break up pieces, until meat is no longer pink.

3. Put gravy mix in a 2-cup glass measure. Gradually stir in cold water until mixture reaches the 1½-cup mark. Pour into skillet. Add remaining ingredients except sour cream. Stir to blend.

4. Bring to a boil and boil 3 to 4 minutes, until vegetables are crisp-tender and sauce has thickened. Remove from heat. Cool slightly, then stir in sour cream. Spoon over the noodles and serve.

Makes 4 servings. Per serving: 363 calories, 36 grams protein, 17 grams carbohydrate, 16 grams fat, 117 milligrams cholesterol, 737 milligrams sodium

Turkey Picadillo

1⅓ cups water
¾ teaspoon salt
1⅓ cups 5-minute rice
1 tablespoon olive oil
1 pound ground turkey
1½ teaspoons ground cumin
1 can (14½ to 16 ounces)
    stewed tomatoes
¼ cup raisins
¼ cup small pimiento-stuffed
    green olives
1 tablespoon tomato ketchup

1. Bring water and ½ teaspoon of the salt to a boil in a medium-size saucepan over high heat. Stir in rice. Cover, remove from heat and set aside.

2. Heat oil in a large skillet over high heat. Crumble in turkey, season with cumin and cook 5 minutes, stirring often to break up pieces, until meat is no longer pink.

3. Stir in tomatoes, raisins, olives, ketchup and remaining ¼ teaspoon salt until well blended.

4. Bring to a boil. Reduce heat to low and simmer 5 minutes, until slightly thickened and bubbly. Serve over the rice.

Makes 4 servings. Per serving: 407 calories, 36 grams protein, 34 grams carbohydrate, 13 grams fat, 111 milligrams cholesterol, 666 milligrams sodium

Turkey and Bell-Pepper Hash

Transfer potato patties from freezer to refrigerator the night before to thaw.

2 tablespoons vegetable oil
1 pound ground turkey
1 medium-size red bell pepper,
   cut in strips
3 frozen shredded potato patties (from
   a 15-ounce package of 6), thawed
1 cup frozen Italian green beans
½ cup frozen or fresh chopped onion
½ teaspoon salt
¼ teaspoon pepper, or to taste

1. Heat oil in a large nonstick skillet over high heat. Crumble in turkey, add bell-pepper strips and cook 5 minutes, stirring often to break up pieces, until meat is no longer pink.

2. Break potato patties in small chunks. Add to turkey with remaining ingredients. Mix well.

3. Press hash into a flat patty with the back of a broad spatula and cook 3 minutes, until underside is browned.

4. Turn hash (no need to turn it in one piece); press flat again and continue cooking 4 minutes longer, until heated through and bottom is crisp. Transfer to a heated platter and serve.

Makes 4 servings. Per serving: 403 calories, 35 grams protein, 23 grams carbohydrate, 24 grams fat, 111 milligrams cholesterol, 635 milligrams sodium

Turkey and Bell-Pepper Hash

In the Pot

Warm up your family or friends on cold winter evenings with these hearty stews and old-fashioned potpies.

Ginger-Garlic-Tomato Chicken

Great Stews

⏱ **MAKE-AHEAD**
♥ **LOW-CALORIE**

Ginger-Garlic-Tomato Chicken

The chicken skin is removed in this recipe, so brown the meat only until golden or it will become tough. Serve with white rice and steamed broccoli. For best quality, refrigerate this stew no longer than two days; it freezes well for longer storage.

- 4 chicken thighs (about 1⅓ pounds), skin and visible fat removed
- ½ teaspoon salt
- ¼ teaspoon pepper
- 1 tablespoon olive oil
- 1 can (28 ounces) tomatoes, drained
- 2 tablespoons grated fresh gingerroot
- 2 tablespoons minced fresh garlic
- 1¼ teaspoons granulated sugar
- ⅛ teaspoon crushed red-pepper flakes
- ½ cup loosely packed fresh cilantro leaves or Italian parsley

1. Season chicken with salt and pepper.

2. Heat oil in a Dutch oven or a medium-size heavy skillet over medium heat. Add chicken and cook 4 to 5 minutes per side, until light golden brown. Remove to a plate with a slotted spoon.

3. Add remaining ingredients except cilantro to Dutch oven. Raise heat to medium-high and cook 3 to 4 minutes, stirring to break up tomatoes, until sauce is thickened.

4. Return chicken to Dutch oven and spoon sauce over top. Bring to a boil. Reduce heat to low. Cover and simmer 25 to 30 minutes, stirring sauce and turning chicken two or three times, until chicken is very tender. Just before serving, sprinkle with cilantro.

Makes 4 servings. Per serving: 188 calories, 19 grams protein, 12 grams carbohydrate, 7 grams fat, 72 milligrams cholesterol, 673 milligrams sodium

⏱ **MAKE-AHEAD**

Quick Chicken-and-Bean Stew

This recipe makes a big pot of stew, so freeze half for another dinner.

- ½ cup all-purpose flour
- ¼ teaspoon salt
- ¼ teaspoon pepper
- 16 chicken thighs (about 4 pounds), skin and visible fat removed
- 3 tablespoons vegetable oil
- 1 pound sweet Italian sausage links (about 5), cut in 1-inch pieces
- 1½ cups finely chopped onions
- 1 bag (16 ounces) frozen chopped collard greens or frozen chopped kale, unthawed
- 2 cans (16 ounces each) small white beans, such as navy or cannellini beans, drained
- 1 can (16 ounces) stewed tomatoes
- 1⅔ cups chicken broth or water
- 1 teaspoon dried rosemary leaves

1. Mix flour, salt and pepper on a sheet of waxed paper. Coat chicken in flour mixture. Reserve remaining flour mixture.

2. Heat oil in a Dutch oven over medium heat. Add chicken in two batches and cook until browned. Remove to a bowl.

3. Add sausage to Dutch oven and cook 3 to 5 minutes, stirring occasionally, until lightly browned all over. Remove to bowl with chicken.

4. Add onions to Dutch oven and cook 5 to 7 minutes, until tender. Stir in remaining flour mixture and the collard greens. Cook 2 minutes, stirring constantly to break up greens. Add remaining ingredients, including chicken and sausage, and stir to mix well.

5. Bring to a boil over high heat. Reduce heat to low. Cover and simmer 25 to 30 minutes, stirring twice, until chicken is fork-tender and no longer pink in the center. Transfer to a heated platter and serve.

Makes 8 servings. Per serving (with broth): 805 calories, 73 grams protein, 34 grams carbohydrate, 41 grams fat, 203 milligrams cholesterol, 968 milligrams sodium

Chicken with Dumplings Olé

Serve this hearty main dish with bowls of toppings: sour cream, chopped cilantro, olives, green onions and shredded Cheddar cheese.

 3 cans (14½ ounces each)
   chicken broth
1½ pounds chicken breasts or thighs,
   skin and visible fat removed
 1 cup diced onion
 1 cup diced celery
 1 teaspoon salt
 1 teaspoon garlic powder
½ teaspoon pepper
 2 cups cubed peeled potatoes
 1 cup sliced carrots
 1 can (14 to 15½ ounces) corn
   kernels, drained
 1 can (8 ounces) tomato sauce
 1 cup mild or medium-spicy salsa
 1 can (3 to 3½ ounces) chopped mild
   green chiles, undrained
¼ cup chopped fresh cilantro
½ cup all-purpose flour
½ cup cold water

Corn Dumplings

 1 cup all-purpose flour
½ cup cornmeal
 2 teaspoons baking powder
½ teaspoon salt
 1 large egg
½ cup milk
 2 tablespoons butter or margarine,
   melted

1. To make chicken: Bring broth to a boil in a covered Dutch oven over high heat. Add chicken, onion, celery, salt, garlic powder and pepper. Reduce heat to medium-low and simmer 45 minutes, until chicken is very tender. Remove chicken with a slotted spoon to a bowl. Let cool.

2. Add potatoes, carrots, half the corn (reserve remainder for dumplings), the tomato sauce, salsa, undrained chiles and cilantro to liquid in Dutch oven. Bring to a boil over high heat.

3. Reduce heat to low. Cover and cook 20 minutes, until vegetables are almost tender.

4. Pull chicken from bones and cut or tear into bite-size pieces.

5. Mix flour and water in a small bowl until well blended. Stir into stew. Add chicken to stew.

6. Meanwhile, make dumplings: Mix all dumpling ingredients, including the reserved corn, in a medium-size bowl.

7. Drop dumpling batter in 8 heaping tablespoons around the top of stew. Cover and simmer over medium heat about 18 minutes, until dumplings are cooked through. Ladle stew into bowls, top each with a dumpling and serve.

Makes 8 servings. Per serving (with chicken breasts): 391 calories, 31 grams protein, 48 grams carbohydrate, 9 grams fat, 94 milligrams cholesterol with butter, 85 milligrams cholesterol with margarine, 1,652 milligrams sodium

Country-Style Drumsticks

 2 tablespoons olive oil
12 chicken drumsticks (about 3
   pounds)
 1 *each* small yellow, red and green
   bell pepper, cut in thin strips
   (about 1½ cups)
 1 large onion, thinly sliced
   (about 1½ cups)
 4 ounces mushrooms, sliced
   (about 1½ cups)
 1 teaspoon dried basil leaves
½ teaspoon dried oregano leaves
¾ teaspoon salt
¼ teaspoon pepper
½ cup chicken broth
½ cup dry white wine or additional
   chicken broth

1. Heat oil in a Dutch oven over medium-high heat. Add chicken and brown, in two batches if necessary. Remove to a plate.

2. Add peppers, onion and mushrooms to Dutch oven. Cook 4 to 5 minutes, stirring occasionally to scrape up browned bits, until vegetables are crisp-tender.

3. Return chicken to Dutch oven. Spoon vegetables over top and sprinkle with basil, oregano, salt and pepper. Pour in broth and wine.

4. Bring to a boil. Reduce heat to low. Cover and simmer 20 to 25 minutes, stirring occasionally, until chicken is tender. Serve from Dutch oven or transfer to a heated serving platter.

Makes 6 servings. Per serving (with wine): 371 calories, 43 grams protein, 7 grams carbohydrate, 18 grams fat, 117 milligrams cholesterol, 516 milligrams sodium

Dutch-Oven Dinners

Historically, Dutch ovens were covered stewing pots that hung by a handle over the fireplace or sat right in the coals. Here we refer to a large, heavy pot or casserole with a tight-fitting lid.

Chicken Paprikash

2¼ cups water
2 chicken-bouillon cubes or 2 teaspoons instant broth granules
2 cups frozen or fresh chopped onions
2 tablespoons tomato paste
4 teaspoons paprika (use hot Hungarian paprika for a spicy stew)
2 cups bow-tie pasta (4 ounces)
8 chicken thighs (about 2 pounds), skinned

1. Heat water and bouillon cubes in a Dutch oven over high heat.

2. When liquid comes to a boil, stir in onions, tomato paste and paprika.

3. When liquid returns to a boil, stir in pasta. Add chicken to Dutch oven. Let boil about 1 minute.

4. Reduce heat to low. Cover and simmer 35 to 40 minutes, until chicken is fork-tender and no longer pink in the center. Ladle into soup bowls and serve.

Makes 4 servings. Per serving: 359 calories, 40 grams protein, 28 grams carbohydrate, 13 grams fat, 107 milligrams cholesterol, 591 milligrams sodium

Chicken Paprikash

⏱ MAKE-AHEAD
Braised Chicken Legs with Red Wine and Bacon

Slices of French bread—lightly toasted, rubbed with a cut clove of garlic and sprinkled with grated Parmesan cheese—complement this hearty dish. This stew is even better the next day.

6 strips thick-sliced bacon, cut crosswise in ½-inch-thick pieces
½ cup all-purpose flour
1½ teaspoons salt
1 teaspoon pepper plus additional pepper
6 *each* chicken drumsticks and thighs (about 4 pounds)
3 tablespoons vegetable oil
2 medium-size leeks, white parts only, cut in 1-inch lengths, rinsed well
1 cup chicken broth
1 cup dry red wine or 1 cup additional chicken broth
2 tablespoons tomato paste
¾ teaspoon dried tarragon leaves

1. Cook bacon in a Dutch oven over medium-low heat until crisp. Remove from heat. Remove bacon with a slotted spoon to paper towels to drain.

2. Mix flour, salt and the 1 teaspoon pepper on a sheet of waxed paper. Coat chicken in flour mixture.

3. Add oil to bacon drippings in Dutch oven and heat over medium-high heat. Add chicken without crowding, in batches if necessary, and brown on all sides. Remove chicken to a plate.

4. Drain off all but 1 tablespoon pan drippings. Reduce heat to medium-low. Add leeks to Dutch oven and cook about 4 minutes, stirring once or twice, until lightly browned. Add broth and wine, stirring to scrape up browned bits. Bring to a boil over high heat.

5. Return browned chicken to Dutch oven. Reduce heat to low. Cover and simmer about 35 minutes, until chicken is fork-tender. Remove chicken to a heated serving dish.

6. Skim fat from pan juices. Stir in tomato paste, tarragon and pepper to taste. Bring to a boil; boil 3 minutes, until slightly thickened. Spoon over chicken, sprinkle with bacon and serve.

Makes 6 servings. Per serving (with wine): 470 calories, 48 grams protein, 12 grams carbohydrate, 23 grams fat, 157 milligrams cholesterol, 789 milligrams sodium

Spanish-Style Chicken and Broccoli

Roasted red peppers add the Latin touch.

2 tablespoons vegetable oil
1½ pounds chicken drumsticks
1½ pounds chicken thighs
2 teaspoons minced fresh garlic
1 cup uncooked long-grain white rice
2¾ cups hot chicken broth
¾ teaspoon turmeric or ¼ teaspoon powdered saffron
1 teaspoon dried oregano leaves
1 small bay leaf
1 bunch broccoli (about 1½ pounds), tough stems removed, separated into florets and tender stems diagonally cut in ¼-inch slices
1 cup frozen pearl onions
½ cup drained roasted red peppers (from a jar), cut in strips

1. Heat oil in a Dutch oven over medium-high heat. Add half the chicken at a time and brown well on all sides. Remove with a slotted spoon to paper towels to drain.

2. Reduce heat to medium and add garlic and rice to Dutch oven. Cook until rice is lightly browned, stirring constantly.

3. Stir in 2¼ cups of the hot chicken broth, the turmeric, oregano and bay leaf. Bring to a boil. Cover, reduce heat to low and simmer 10 minutes, stirring once.

4. Add browned chicken, broccoli stems and pearl onions. Cover and simmer 15 minutes longer.

5. Add broccoli florets, peppers and remaining ½ cup broth. Cover and simmer 10 minutes.

6. Uncover and cook 5 minutes longer, until liquid is absorbed and chicken is no longer pink in the center. Discard bay leaf and serve.

Makes 6 servings. Per serving: 450 calories, 39 grams protein, 34 grams carbohydrate, 12 grams fat, 110 milligrams cholesterol, 447 milligrams sodium

⏱ MAKE-AHEAD
Stewed Chicken with Rice and Turnip Greens

You can use kale, mustard greens or plain turnip greens instead of the diced turnips and greens. This dish improves on standing; leftovers are twice as delicious.

2 tablespoons olive or vegetable oil
1 medium-size onion, thinly sliced (about ½ cup)
1 teaspoon minced fresh garlic
8 chicken thighs (about 2½ pounds), skin and visible fat removed
1 package (10 ounces) frozen diced turnips and greens, thawed and drained
1 cup uncooked long-grain white rice
2 cups chicken broth
1 tablespoon Dijon mustard
1 teaspoon salt
½ teaspoon poultry seasoning
½ teaspoon pepper
1 large ripe tomato, chopped (about 1 cup)

1. Heat oil in a Dutch oven over medium-high heat. Add onion and garlic and cook 3 to 4 minutes, stirring twice, until onion is nearly tender.

2. Push onion to one side of Dutch oven. Add chicken and cook 2 to 3 minutes per side, until outside is no longer pink.

3. Stir in turnips and greens, rice, broth, mustard, salt, poultry seasoning and pepper. Bring to a boil. Reduce heat to low, cover and simmer 10 minutes.

4. Stir in tomato. Cover and continue to simmer 10 to 12 minutes, until the rice is tender and chicken is no longer pink in the center. Transfer to a heated platter and serve.

Makes 4 servings. Per serving: 445 calories, 38 grams protein, 44 grams carbohydrate, 12 grams fat, 116 milligrams cholesterol, 992 milligrams sodium

Potpies

Could anything be more soul-satisfying? One version here takes a bit of time, the other is an easy-fix dish; both are delicious.

★ SPECIAL—AND WORTH IT
✳ MICROWAVE

Old-fashioned Chicken Potpie

The real thing! Both the creamy filling and the biscuit dough are made from scratch.

Filling

1	broiler-fryer chicken (about 3 pounds), quartered
4	cups chicken broth
2	medium-size carrots, halved crosswise
2	medium-size onions
1	bay leaf (2 inches long)
6	ounces small mushrooms, halved (about 2 cups)
2	medium-size stalks celery, halved crosswise
3	tablespoons butter or margarine
¼	cup plus 2 teaspoons all-purpose flour
½	cup heavy cream
1	teaspoon poultry seasoning
1	teaspoon salt
¼	teaspoon pepper
1	cup frozen green peas

Biscuit Dough

1½	cups all-purpose flour
2	teaspoons baking powder
1¼	teaspoons granulated sugar
¼	teaspoon salt
¼	cup plus 2 teaspoons solid vegetable shortening
½	cup milk

1. To make filling: Combine chicken, broth, carrots, onions and bay leaf in a Dutch oven over medium-high heat. Bring to a boil. Reduce heat to medium, cover and simmer 20 minutes.

2. Skim foam from surface. Add mushrooms and celery. Cover and simmer 15 minutes longer, until chicken and vegetables are fork-tender.

3. Remove vegetables to a cutting board. Let cool slightly. Coarsely chop onion; slice carrots and celery. Leave chicken in broth until cool enough to handle. Remove skin; pull meat from bones in large pieces. (You should have about 3 cups.) Strain broth; skim off fat. Measure out 2 cups. (Refrigerate the rest for another use.)

4. Have a deep 2-quart casserole ready. Melt butter in same Dutch oven over low heat. Stir in flour until smooth. Let mixture bubble about 3 minutes, stirring often to prevent browning.

5. Gradually stir in 2 cups reserved broth and the cream. Cook over medium heat, stirring constantly, until simmering and thickened. Stir in poultry seasoning, salt, pepper, peas, vegetables and chicken. Pour into casserole.

6. To make biscuit dough: Mix flour, baking powder, sugar and salt in a medium-size bowl. Cut in shortening with a pastry blender or two knives until mixture resembles coarse crumbs. Stir in milk and beat with a wooden spoon until a soft dough forms.

7. Turn dough out onto a lightly floured surface and roll or pat to ½-inch thickness.

8. Heat oven to 400°F.

9. Cut dough with a floured 2- to 2½-inch biscuit cutter. Arrange biscuits over filling. (Put any extra biscuits on a baking sheet.) Bake 20 minutes, until biscuits are well browned.

Makes 6 servings. Per serving: 540 calories, 31 grams protein, 41 grams carbohydrate, 27 grams fat, 121 milligrams cholesterol with butter, 103 milligrams cholesterol with margarine, 1,231 milligrams sodium

Microwave Method: Bake biscuits in a conventional oven on a baking sheet as directed while filling cooks in the microwave. To make filling: Cut carrots and celery in 2-inch pieces, onions in ½-inch-thick wedges. Place in a deep 3- to 4-quart microwave-safe casserole; add bay leaf and mushrooms. Arrange chicken on top, with thickest parts toward outer edge of casserole. Pour 2½ cups broth over chicken. Cover with a lid or vented plastic wrap. Microwave on high 10 minutes, rotating dish ¼ turn once. Rearrange chicken pieces, bringing those from center to outer edge. Cover and microwave on high 7 to 9 minutes longer, rotating dish once, until chicken is opaque and vegetables almost tender. Let stand 20 minutes. When cool enough to handle, prepare chicken, vegetables and broth as directed. Melt butter in a deep 2-quart microwave-safe casserole. Whisk in flour, then 2 cups of the broth from chicken and the cream. Microwave on high 6 to 8 minutes, stirring twice, until thickened. Stir in chicken, vegetables and remaining ingredients. Cover and microwave on high 2 to 3 minutes, until peas are hot. Let stand 5 minutes. Top with hot biscuits.

Old-fashioned Chicken Potpie

Turkey Potpie

If you have leftover chicken, you can use that instead of the turkey. This potpie is a stream-lined version, yet every bit as hearty and delicious as the one on the previous page. It makes good use of convenience foods such as gravy mix, frozen vegetables, canned mushrooms and refrigerated biscuits.

1½ cups milk
 1 packet (⅞ ounce) chicken-gravy
    mix
 1 pound cooked turkey, cut in ½-
    inch cubes (about 2½ cups)
 1 package (10 ounces) frozen mixed
    baby carrots, peas and pearl
    onions
 1 jar (4½ ounces) button
    mushrooms, drained
 1 teaspoon poultry seasoning
⅛ teaspoon pepper
 1 can (7.5 ounces) refrigerated
    buttermilk biscuits
For garnish: fresh sage sprigs

1. Heat oven to 400°F. Have a 9-inch deep-dish pie plate ready.

2. Stir milk and gravy mix in a small saucepan until smooth. Bring to a boil over medium-high heat, stirring constantly. Reduce heat to medium-low and simmer 1 minute, stirring constantly, until sauce is thickened.

3. Put turkey, mixed vegetables, mushrooms, poultry seasoning and pepper in pie plate. Pour hot sauce into pie plate and toss lightly to mix.

4. Bake 5 minutes to heat through.

5. Place a border of biscuits, ½ inch apart, over filling. Bake 8 to 10 minutes, until biscuits are golden and filling is bubbly. Garnish with sage sprigs and serve.

Makes 4 servings. Per serving: 464 calories, 45 grams protein, 41 grams carbohydrate, 12 grams fat, 114 milligrams cholesterol, 2,182 milligrams sodium

59

Braised or Stewed Turkey

Begin by browning the poultry to lock in flavor and juices. Add liquid and simmer for an easy, hearty dinner.

Turkey Stew with Corn and Bell Peppers

Rice is nice with this fast-cooking stew. To brown the turkey properly, heat oil until hot but not smoking, and add meat in a single layer, leaving a little space between each piece. Adding too much meat at one time will lower the temperature of the oil and prevent browning. For dessert, cut ripe pears into wedges; drizzle with maple syrup and sprinkle with cinnamon.

- ½ cup all-purpose flour
- 1½ teaspoons salt plus additional salt
- 1 teaspoon pepper plus additional pepper
- 4 large turkey thighs (about 4 pounds), skinned, boned and cut in 1½-inch chunks
- ⅓ cup vegetable oil
- 1 large red bell pepper, cut in ½-inch dice
- 1 can (8¼ ounces) corn kernels, drained
- ½ cup thinly sliced white part of green onions
- 2 cups chicken broth
- 3 tablespoons thinly sliced green-onion tops

1. Mix flour, the 1½ teaspoons salt and the 1 teaspoon pepper on a sheet of waxed paper. Coat turkey in flour mixture, shaking off excess flour.

2. Heat oil in a Dutch oven over medium-high heat until hot but not smoking. Add turkey, in batches if necessary, and brown well. Transfer browned turkey with a slotted spoon to a plate.

3. Reduce heat to medium-low. Drain off all but 1 tablespoon drippings from Dutch oven. Add bell pepper, corn and white part of green onions to Dutch oven.

4. Cook about 5 minutes, until bell pepper is crisp-tender. Remove vegetables with a slotted spoon to a small bowl and reserve.

5. Add broth, stirring to scrape up browned bits. Raise heat to high and bring to a boil.

6. Return browned meat to Dutch oven. Reduce heat to low. Cover and simmer about 30 minutes.

7. Taste; season with salt and pepper and add additional broth if necessary. Stir in reserved vegetables and simmer 5 minutes longer. Ladle into bowls, sprinkle each serving with green-onion tops and serve.

Makes 6 servings. Per serving: 452 calories, 54 grams protein, 14 grams carbohydrate, 19 grams fat, 176 milligrams cholesterol, 1,005 milligrams sodium

Turkey Stew with Corn and Bell Peppers

Braised Turkey Thighs in Sweet-and-Sour Cherry Sauce

Baked sweet potatoes or a mashed winter squash such as butternut or acorn is a good accompaniment.

3 tablespoons vegetable oil
4 turkey thighs (about 8 ounces each)
1 package (about 1 ounce)
    white-sauce mix
1 cup beef broth
3 tablespoons cider vinegar
2 tablespoons honey or packed
    brown sugar
3 cloves garlic
1 bay leaf (about 1 inch long)
1 teaspoon dried sage leaves
3 whole cloves
Pepper to taste
1 can (16½ ounces) pitted dark
    cherries in syrup, undrained

1. Heat oil in a Dutch oven over medium-high heat. Add turkey thighs and brown on all sides. Remove thighs with a slotted spoon to a plate. Drain off all but 1 tablespoon drippings from Dutch oven.

2. Stir in remaining ingredients except cherries and turkey until well blended. Bring to a boil over high heat.

3. Add turkey thighs skin-side up and reduce heat to low. Cover and simmer 1½ hours or until turkey is fork-tender.

4. Remove thighs to a foil-lined broiler pan.

5. Turn on broiler. Skim fat from surface of sauce and discard bay leaf. Add cherries, bring to a boil over medium-high heat and boil 3 minutes, until sauce thickens.

6. Meanwhile, place turkey under broiler briefly to crisp the skin.

7. Spoon some sauce with cherries onto a heated platter and arrange thighs on top. Serve remaining sauce on the side.

Makes 4 servings. Per serving (with honey): 585 calories, 37 grams protein, 38 grams carbohydrate, 27 grams fat, 135 milligrams cholesterol, 459 milligrams sodium

🕐 **MAKE-AHEAD**

Braised Turkey with Italian Sausage

This is delicious served over pasta or with garlic bread. Start your meal with a cold antipasto; arrange celery, carrots, roasted red peppers, artichoke hearts, pepperoncini and olives on a platter. Drizzle with olive oil and a good-quality red-wine vinegar. This stew improves with age.

1 pound sweet Italian sausage,
    removed from casings
½ cup all-purpose flour
1½ teaspoons salt plus additional salt
1 teaspoon pepper plus additional
    pepper
4 pounds turkey legs and thighs
⅓ cup vegetable oil
2 medium-size onions, minced
    (about 1 cup)
About 1¼ cups chicken broth
¾ cup canned crushed tomatoes
½ cup chopped fresh parsley

1. Crumble sausage meat into a Dutch oven. Cook over medium-high heat 10 minutes, stirring occasionally, until meat is browned and fully cooked. Remove with a slotted spoon to a plate. Drain all fat from Dutch oven.

2. Mix flour, the 1½ teaspoons salt and the 1 teaspoon pepper on a sheet of waxed paper. Coat turkey in flour mixture, shaking off excess.

3. Heat oil in Dutch oven over medium-high heat until hot but not smoking. Add turkey in batches and brown well. Remove to a plate.

4. Drain off all but 1 tablespoon pan drippings. Reduce heat to medium-low. Add onions to Dutch oven and cook about 5 minutes, stirring once or twice, until lightly browned.

5. Add broth, tomatoes and parsley, stirring to scrape up browned bits. Bring to a boil over high heat.

6. Return browned turkey to Dutch oven. Sprinkle with cooked sausage. Reduce heat to low. Cover and simmer 45 minutes, turning turkey pieces and stirring sauce once.

7. Add additional broth if too thick and season to taste with salt and pepper. Cover and simmer 45 minutes longer, until turkey is fork-tender and sauce is slightly thickened. Ladle into bowls and serve.

Makes 8 servings. Per serving: 419 calories, 46 grams protein, 8 grams carbohydrate, 18 grams fat, 152 milligrams cholesterol, 817 milligrams sodium

Wingding Gumbo with Sweet Potatoes
and Red Bell Peppers

🕐 MAKE-AHEAD

Wingding Gumbo with Sweet Potatoes and Red Bell Peppers

½ cup olive or vegetable oil
8 turkey drumettes (about 10 ounces each)
½ cup plus 1 tablespoon all-purpose flour
4 cups beef broth
1 teaspoon dried thyme leaves
2 small bay leaves
2 teaspoons minced fresh garlic
½ teaspoon salt
¼ teaspoon pepper, or to taste
3 medium-size sweet potatoes (about 1 pound), peeled and quartered
2 large red bell peppers (about 1 pound), cut in 2-inch strips
1 cup 2-inch pieces green onions

1. Heat 3 tablespoons of the oil in a Dutch oven over medium-high heat. Add drumettes and brown on all sides. Remove to a plate.

2. Add remaining oil to Dutch oven and heat until hot but not smoking. Stir in flour until smooth and frothy. Let bubble about 3 minutes, stirring frequently, until reddish-brown.

3. Stir in broth and cook until thickened, stirring constantly.

4. Add thyme, bay leaves, garlic, salt, pepper and drumettes to Dutch oven. Reduce heat to medium-low. Cover and simmer 1 hour.

5. Remove from heat. Skim fat from surface of sauce. Add sweet potatoes, bell peppers and green onions to Dutch oven. Cover and simmer about 25 minutes, until meat and potatoes are tender. Discard bay leaves, transfer to a heated serving dish and serve.

Makes 4 servings. Per serving: 815 calories, 49 grams protein, 35 grams carbohydrate, 53 grams fat, 185 milligrams cholesterol, 1,205 milligrams sodium

Starting with Cooked

These recipes offer new and easy ways to use up Thanksgiving leftovers, but don't wait until November to make them. You can always buy cooked turkey at the deli.

✳ MICROWAVE

New Orleans Turkey-Okra Stew

1 tablespoon vegetable oil
1 cup chopped onion
1 medium-size red or green bell pepper, coarsely chopped (about 1¼ cups)
1 teaspoon minced fresh garlic
3 tablespoons all-purpose flour
3 cups chicken broth
1 package (10 ounces) frozen sliced okra
4 ounces fully cooked ham, diced (about ¾ cup)
1½ teaspoons dried thyme leaves
½ teaspoon ground red pepper
2 cups shredded cooked turkey

1. Heat oil in a 3-quart saucepan or a Dutch oven over medium heat. Stir in onion, bell pepper and garlic. Cook 5 minutes, stirring occasionally, until onion is tender.

2. Sprinkle in flour and stir until blended.

3. Add broth, okra, ham, thyme and ground red pepper to saucepan. Raise heat to medium-high. Cover and bring to a boil. Reduce heat to low and simmer uncovered 10 to 15 minutes, stirring occasionally, until okra is tender, mixture has thickened and flavors have blended.

4. Stir in turkey and simmer 1 minute, until hot, then transfer to a serving dish and serve.

Makes 4 servings. Per serving: 333 calories, 34 grams protein, 17 grams carbohydrate, 14 grams fat, 98 milligrams cholesterol, 800 milligrams sodium

Microwave Method: Put oil, onion, bell pepper and garlic in a 2-quart microwave-safe casserole. Cover and cook on high 3 to 4 minutes, stirring twice, until vegetables are crisp-tender. Stir in flour and microwave on high 1 minute. Stir in remaining ingredients except turkey. Cover and microwave on high 6 to 8 minutes, stirring twice, until okra is crisp-tender and mixture has thickened slightly. Stir in turkey. Cover and let stand 5 minutes, until turkey is heated through.

Turkey-Stuffing Hot Dish

Give thanks all year round for this easy version of a meal usually reserved for holidays. Serve with cranberry sauce or relish.

1⅔ cups chicken broth
  1 package (6 ounces) diced dried fruit
      and raisins (1½ cups)
 12 ounces thin-sliced turkey-breast
      cutlets, cut in 2-inch-long, ¼-
      inch-thick strips (2 cups)
  3 tablespoons corn or peanut oil
  1 teaspoon dried sage leaves,
      crumbled
 ⅛ teaspoon pepper
  1 cup thinly sliced celery
 ⅓ cup thinly sliced green onions
  3 cups (about 5 ounces) packaged
      cubed stuffing mix

1. Mix chicken broth and dried fruit in a 4-cup measure or a medium-size bowl.

2. Mix turkey, 1 tablespoon of the oil, the sage and pepper in a medium-size bowl.

3. Place a Dutch oven over high heat about 3 minutes, until very hot. Add 1 tablespoon of the oil. Tilt Dutch oven to coat bottom with oil. Add turkey mixture and stir-fry 1 to 1½ minutes, until turkey is no longer pink. Spoon into a large bowl.

4. Heat remaining 1 tablespoon oil in Dutch oven. Add celery and stir-fry 1 minute. Add green onions and stir-fry 30 seconds, until green onions are wilted and celery is crisp-tender. Add to bowl with turkey.

5. Put broth mixture in Dutch oven and bring to a boil, scraping up browned bits from bottom. Add stuffing mix. Stir until all broth is absorbed.

6. Return turkey and vegetables to Dutch oven. Stir 1 minute, until blended and hot, then serve from Dutch oven or transfer to a serving dish.

Makes 4 servings. Per serving: 537 calories, 35 grams protein, 60 grams carbohydrate, 18 grams fat, 71 milligrams cholesterol, 995 milligrams sodium

⏱ MAKE-AHEAD

Turkey Chili

  2 tablespoons olive oil
1½ cups chopped sweet red or
      white onions
  1 cup frozen or fresh chopped green
      bell peppers
  2 tablespoons chili powder
1½ teaspoons minced fresh garlic
  1 can (16 ounces) tomatoes,
      undrained, cut up
  1 can (16 ounces) vegetarian-style
      baked beans
 ½ cup chicken broth
  2 cups diced cooked turkey
 ½ teaspoon salt

1. Heat oil in a large saucepan over high heat. Add 1¼ cups of the onions and the bell peppers. Cook, stirring occasionally, until onions are tender.

2. Add chili powder and garlic and stir 30 seconds. Add tomatoes with their juice, beans and chicken broth. Cover and bring to a boil. Reduce heat to medium and simmer 5 minutes.

3. Stir in turkey and salt. Simmer uncovered 2 to 3 minutes, until turkey is hot. Ladle into bowls and top servings with remaining ¼ cup chopped onions.

Makes 4 servings. Per serving: 353 calories, 29 grams protein, 37 grams carbohydrate, 12 grams fat, 54 milligrams cholesterol, 1,087 milligrams sodium

Turkey Chili

In
the
Oven

Dinner's in the oven with these crispy-skinned roast chickens and turkeys and complete casseroles. We'll help you get the Thanksgiving bird on the table, too, with recipes and hints tailored for the busy cook.

Parslied Roast Chicken

Perfect Roasts

Parslied Roast Chicken

Forty minutes, that's all it takes to roast this simple and delicious chicken. Turn it just once, and don't baste at all. Then whisk up a superb sauce right in the same pan from the specially seasoned juices.

1 broiler-fryer chicken (about
    2½ pounds)
½ teaspoon salt
½ teaspoon pepper, or to taste
2 cloves garlic, crushed
½ cup minced fresh parsley
⅓ cup minced green onions
2 tablespoons butter or margarine
¼ cup dry white wine

1. Heat oven to 400°F. Heavily oil a large oven-proof skillet or a shallow range-top baking dish.

2. Remove giblets package from chicken. Pull off excess fat. Rinse chicken inside and out and dry with paper towels. Season with salt and pepper. Rub cavity with half the garlic and 1 tablespoon each of the parsley and green onions. Tie legs together with white string and tuck wing tips under the back. Place breast-side down in prepared skillet.

3. Roast 15 minutes. Turn gently with a wooden spoon, being careful not to tear the breast skin. Roast 25 minutes longer, until a drumstick moves easily and the juices run clear yellow with no tinges of pink when the thigh is pierced.

4. Transfer chicken to a cutting board. Let stand 5 minutes.

5. Carve chicken and arrange on a heated platter, reserving carving juices. Cover loosely with foil and keep warm.

6. Add butter and remaining green onions to chicken drippings in skillet. Cook over high heat, stirring frequently, until onions are tender. Add remaining garlic, the wine and the carving juices. Bring to a boil, stirring to loosen browned bits in skillet. Boil 1 to 2 minutes, until slightly reduced.

7. Stir in remaining parsley and cook just until hot. Spoon sauce over chicken and serve.

Makes 4 servings. Per serving: 310 calories, 36 grams protein, 2 grams carbohydrate, 15 grams fat, 181 milligrams cholesterol with butter, 163 milligrams cholesterol with margarine, 352 milligrams sodium

♥ LOW-CALORIE
Succulent Roast Chicken

To go with the chicken, bake potatoes or an acorn squash in the hot oven. You also might want to bake an easy dessert, like baked apples or a fruit crisp, at the same time.

1 broiler-fryer chicken (about
    3 pounds)
¾ teaspoon salt
¼ teaspoon pepper
2 small stalks celery, cut in
    2-inch chunks
4 parsley sprigs
1 tablespoon sliced green onion
½ teaspoon crumbled dried
    thyme leaves
1 small onion, cut in chunks
1 tablespoon vegetable oil
¾ cup water

1. Heat oven to 400°F. Have a 13x9-inch baking pan ready.

2. Remove neck and giblets from chicken; reserve for soup or other use. Rinse chicken. Drain and pat dry with paper towels.

3. Season chicken inside and out with ½ teaspoon of the salt and the pepper. Put half the celery chunks, the parsley sprigs and green onion in chicken cavity. Sprinkle chicken with thyme. Tie legs together with white string and tuck wing tips under the back.

4. Add remaining celery and the cut-up onion to baking pan. Put chicken breast-side up on vegetables. Brush with oil.

5. Roast 1 hour, until chicken is golden brown and juices run clear when thigh is pierced. Drain cavity juices into baking pan. Put chicken on a heated platter.

6. Heat vegetables and drippings in baking pan over medium heat 1 minute. Add water and bring to a boil, stirring to scrape up browned bits. Boil 4 minutes, until slightly reduced. Stir in remaining ¼ teaspoon salt. Strain into gravy boat. Skim off fat. Carve chicken and serve with the gravy.

Makes 4 servings chicken and about ¾ cup gravy.
Per serving with 3 tablespoons gravy: 233 calories, 27 grams protein, 5 grams carbohydrate, 11 grams fat, 74 milligrams cholesterol, 775 milligrams sodium

Roast Chicken with Tortilla Stuffing

Look for corn tortillas in your market's refrigerator case.

1 roasting chicken (about 7 pounds)
¼ cup fresh-squeezed or bottled
    lime juice
3 tablespoons vegetable oil
Seven 6-inch corn tortillas, halved and
    cut crosswise in ½-inch-thick
    strips (about 2¼ cups)
1 medium-size red onion, chopped
    (about 1 cup)
1 can (8 ounces) tomato sauce
1 can (4 ounces) chopped green chiles,
    undrained
2 tablespoons chopped fresh cilantro
    leaves or 1 tablespoon dried
    cilantro, crumbled
½ teaspoon salt
¼ teaspoon pepper
Chunky tomato salsa from a jar
    (optional)

1. Heat oven to 350°F. Have ready a roasting pan and rack.

2. Remove neck and giblets from chicken. Coarsely chop liver. Reserve neck and remaining giblets for soup or other use.

3. Rinse chicken and dry well with paper towels. Brush inside and out with 2 tablespoons of the lime juice.

4. Heat oil in a large skillet over medium heat. Fry tortilla strips in two batches about 2 minutes, stirring once or twice, until lightly browned and crisp. Remove to paper towels to drain.

5. Add onion to skillet and cook until tender.

6. Add liver and cook about 1 minute, stirring constantly, until liver loses its pink color.

7. Remove skillet from heat. Add tortilla strips and remaining ingredients except salsa and stir until blended.

8. Loosely stuff neck and body cavities with tortilla mixture. Secure with skewers. Tie legs together with white string and tuck wing tips under back. Place chicken breast-side up on rack in roasting pan.

9. Roast about 2½ hours, basting once with remaining 2 tablespoons lime juice, until juices run clear when thigh is pierced.

10. Cover loosely with foil; let stand about 15 minutes before carving. Carve chicken and serve with salsa, if desired.

Makes 4 servings plus leftovers. Per 4 ounces cooked chicken with ¼ of the stuffing (without salsa): 435 calories, 38 grams protein, 33 grams carbohydrate, 17 grams fat, 96 milligrams cholesterol, 636 milligrams sodium

Microwave Method: Spread half the tortilla strips on a double thickness of paper towels in oven. Microwave on high 2½ to 3½ minutes, until crisp but not browned. Repeat with remaining strips on fresh towels. Put onion in a 3-quart microwave-safe bowl. Add 1 tablespoon oil; microwave uncovered on high 3 to 4 minutes, stirring once, until onion is tender. Add liver; microwave on high 30 to 60 seconds, until liver loses its pink color. Assemble stuffing as directed. Brush chicken inside and out with 2 tablespoons of the lime juice. Spoon stuffing into chicken cavities. Secure with wooden skewers. Sprinkle surface of chicken with paprika to add color, if you wish. Put breast-side down on a microwave-safe roasting rack with sides or in a 12x8x2-inch baking dish. Microwave uncovered on high 20 minutes. Turn chicken breast-side up; brush with the remaining lime juice. Microwave 20 minutes longer, until chicken is tender and drumstick moves easily. Cover loosely with foil; let stand 20 minutes, until juices run clear when thigh is pierced, carve and serve.

Greek Roast Chicken Oreganato

Serve with rice cooked in chicken broth and garlic-flavored green beans.

- 1 broiler-fryer chicken (about 2½ pounds)
- 1½ teaspoons crumbled dried oregano leaves
- ½ teaspoon salt
- ½ teaspoon pepper, or to taste
- 2 tablespoons olive oil
- 1 tablespoon lemon juice

1. Heat oven to 400°F. Heavily oil a large oven-proof skillet or a shallow range-top baking dish.

2. Remove giblets package from chicken. Pull off excess fat. Rinse chicken inside and out and dry with paper towels. Mix oregano, salt and pepper on a sheet of waxed paper. Sprinkle over chicken and rub inside cavity. Tie legs together with white string and tuck wing tips under the back. Place breast-side down in prepared skillet. Spoon oil over chicken.

3. Roast 15 minutes. Turn gently with a wooden spoon, being careful not to tear the breast skin. Roast 25 minutes longer, until a drumstick moves easily and the juices run clear yellow with no tinges of pink when the thigh is pierced.

4. Transfer chicken to a cutting board. Let stand 5 minutes. Carve chicken and arrange on a heated platter, reserving carving juices. Cover loosely with foil and keep warm.

5. Add carving juices and lemon juice to skillet drippings. Bring to a simmer over medium-high heat, stirring to loosen browned bits in skillet. Spoon juices over chicken and serve.

Makes 4 servings. Per serving: 299 calories, 36 grams protein, 0 grams carbohydrate, 16 grams fat, 163 milligrams cholesterol, 267 milligrams sodium

Roast Chicken Gremolata

Northern Italians call the mixture of lemon peel, garlic and parsley *gremolata* and sprinkle it over ossobuco, their famous veal-shank stew. Serve this chicken with buttered noodles and a spinach or arugula salad.

- 1 broiler-fryer chicken (about 2½ pounds)
- 2 tablespoons minced fresh parsley
- 1 tablespoon olive oil
- 1 tablespoon finely grated lemon peel
- 2 large cloves garlic, crushed
- ½ teaspoon salt
- ½ teaspoon pepper

1. Heat oven to 400°F. Heavily oil a large oven-proof skillet or a shallow range-top baking dish.

2. Remove giblets package from chicken. Pull off excess fat. Rinse chicken inside and out and dry with paper towels.

3. Mix remaining ingredients in a cup and rub over chicken skin and inside cavity. Tie legs together with white string and tuck wing tips under the back. Place breast-side down in prepared skillet.

4. Roast 15 minutes. Turn gently with a wooden spoon, being careful not to tear the breast skin. Roast 25 minutes longer, until a drumstick moves easily and juices run clear yellow with no tinges of pink when the thigh is pierced.

5. Transfer chicken to a cutting board. Let stand 5 minutes. Carve chicken and arrange on a heated platter, reserving carving juices. Cover loosely with foil and keep warm.

6. Add carving juices to chicken drippings in skillet. Bring just to a simmer over medium-high heat, stirring to loosen browned bits in skillet. Spoon over chicken and serve.

Makes 4 servings. Per serving: 271 calories, 36 grams protein, 1 gram carbohydrate, 13 grams fat, 163 milligrams cholesterol, 271 milligrams sodium

Roast Chicken with Matzo Stuffing

Serve with buttered broccoli and glazed carrots.

1 roasting chicken (about 6 pounds)
4 tablespoons vegetable oil
1¾ teaspoons salt
¾ teaspoon pepper
3 matzos
1½ cups water
2 large onions, chopped
1 large tart apple, chopped
1 large egg, lightly beaten
1 tablespoon lemon juice
¼ cup apple juice
2 tablespoons honey

1. Have ready a large shallow roasting pan with a rack.

2. Remove giblets package from chicken. Pull off excess fat. Rinse chicken inside and out and dry with paper towels. Rub chicken skin and cavity with a mixture of 1 tablespoon of the oil, ¾ teaspoon of the salt and ¼ teaspoon of the pepper.

3. Break up matzos in a medium bowl. Pour in water and soak until softened. Pour off water; squeeze excess water from matzos.

4. Heat 2 tablespoons of the oil in a large skillet over medium-high heat. Add onions and cook, stirring occasionally, until lightly browned. Add to soaked matzos. Stir in apple, egg, lemon juice and remaining salt and pepper until blended.

5. Heat oven to 375°F. Loosely stuff chicken-neck cavity. Fasten neck skin to back with skewers. Tuck wing tips under back. Loosely stuff body cavity and close with skewers. Tie legs together with white string. Place breast-side up on rack in roasting pan.

6. Roast 2 hours, untying legs after 1 hour. During last half hour of roasting, baste frequently with a mixture of apple juice, honey and remaining 1 tablespoon oil. (If chicken browns too quickly, cover with a foil tent.) Chicken is done when the skin is browned, a drumstick moves easily and a meat thermometer inserted in the thickest part of thigh (not touching bone) registers 185°F.

7. Remove chicken from oven. Remove skewers. Let chicken stand 15 minutes before carving and serving.

Makes 10 servings. Per serving: 478 calories, 40 grams protein, 18 grams carbohydrate, 26 grams fat, 220 milligrams cholesterol, 593 milligrams sodium

No-Fuss Baked Chicken

No-Fuss Baked Chicken

Serve with herbed rice tossed with chopped fresh parsley, and sautéed cherry tomatoes.

½ cup mayonnaise
¼ cup grated Parmesan cheese
2 tablespoons prepared mustard
4 boned and skinned chicken-breast halves (about 6 ounces each)
⅔ cup cornflake crumbs

1. Heat oven to 400°F. Lightly grease a shallow baking pan.

2. Mix mayonnaise, cheese and mustard in a small bowl. Measure out ⅓ cup and refrigerate.

3. Brush both sides of chicken with the remaining mayonnaise mixture. Coat well with crumbs. Arrange in prepared pan.

4. Bake 20 minutes, until golden brown and fork-tender. Serve with reserved mayonnaise mixture for dipping.

Makes 4 servings. Per serving: 511 calories, 49 grams protein, 13 grams carbohydrate, 28 grams fat, 137 milligrams cholesterol, 533 milligrams sodium

Cut the Cleanup

These recipes inventively seal in the flavors and juices. To clean up, just throw away the wrappings.

Mexican Chicken Dinner

When cooking in foil, cover the food loosely (so that the foil can puff up as steam is created), then double-fold the edges securely to prevent leaks.

> 4 **boned and skinned chicken-breast halves (about 5 ounces each)**
> 2 **teaspoons Mexican dried-herb seasoning**
> Four 4-inch-long sprigs fresh cilantro **or 2 teaspoons dried cilantro**
> 2 **large fresh tomatoes, each sliced in 6 rounds**
> 1½ **cups** *each* **frozen corn kernels and frozen tiny green peas, mixed**
> 1 **lime, sliced in 8 thin rounds**

1. Heat oven to 450°F. Have ready a baking sheet.

2. Tear off four 14x12-inch rectangles of foil. Lightly spray one side of each rectangle with no-stick vegetable spray or brush with oil.

3. Remove the tough white ligament from the underside of each chicken-breast half by scraping along the ligament with a sharp knife. Place chicken on a cutting board and press with palms of hands to flatten evenly.

4. Place a piece of chicken in center of lower half of each foil rectangle. Sprinkle each with ½ teaspoon Mexican seasoning and top with a sprig of cilantro. Arrange three overlapping tomato slices on one side of each chicken breast. Spoon ¾ cup corn-and-pea mixture and 2 lime slices on other side.

5. Fold top of foil over food, bringing side edges of foil together. Turn bottom edge up to meet top edge and make a double fold. Smooth with fingers. Double-fold each side securely.

6. Arrange packets on baking sheet.

7. Bake 12 to 14 minutes, until packets are puffed and chicken is cooked through (see Is It Ready?, right). Remove packets to plates.

8. To open packets, cut a crisscross through the top of foil and turn cut ends back. Remove chicken from packets and serve.

Makes 4 servings. Per serving: 346 calories, 51 grams protein, 23 grams carbohydrate, 5 grams fat, 112 milligrams cholesterol, 299 milligrams sodium

Chicken Breasts with Curry-Chutney Butter

The delicate curry flavor of the chicken goes well with rice and a salad of chopped cucumbers and tomatoes in a dressing of garlic- and mint-flavored sour cream or yogurt.

> 4 **tablespoons butter or margarine, at room temperature**
> 2 **tablespoons mango chutney, chopped**
> 1 **teaspoon curry powder**
> 4 **skinned and boned chicken-breast halves (about 5 ounces each)**

1. Heat oven to 400°F. Have ready a baking sheet.

2. Tear off four 12-inch squares of foil. Lightly coat one side of each square with no-stick vegetable spray or brush lightly with oil.

3. Process or mix butter, chutney and curry powder in a food processor or a small bowl with a wooden spoon until well blended.

4. Remove the tough white ligament from the underside of each chicken-breast half by scraping along the ligament with a sharp knife. Put chicken on a cutting board and press with palms of hands to flatten evenly.

5. Place a chicken breast in center of lower half of each piece of foil. Spread each with ¼ of the butter mixture. Fold top half of foil over chicken, bringing side edges of foil together. Turn bottom edge up to meet top edge and make a double fold. Smooth with fingers. Double-fold each side securely. Arrange packets on baking sheet.

6. Bake 15 minutes, until packets are puffed and chicken is cooked through (see Is It Ready?, below). Remove packets to plates.

7. To open packets, cut a crisscross through top of foil and turn cut ends back. Remove chicken from packets and serve.

Makes 4 servings. Per serving: 363 calories, 45 grams protein, 7 grams carbohydrate, 16 grams fat, 147 milligrams cholesterol with butter, 111 milligrams cholesterol with margarine, 252 milligrams sodium

---

Is It Ready?

Slit top of one packet carefully so that juices don't spill. Chicken should look barely opaque, with just the slightest pink color in the center when pierced with a knife in the thickest part. If the packets need further cooking, cover the slit with a small piece of foil and return to the oven for a few more minutes.

Chicken Breasts Primavera

Chicken Breasts Primavera

A green salad and a crusty loaf of Italian bread are all you need to accompany this dish. Vanilla ice cream with fresh or canned peaches would be delicious for dessert.

6 boned and skinned chicken-breast halves (about 5 ounces each)
¼ teaspoon salt
⅛ teaspoon pepper
1 medium-size red bell pepper, cut in 2½x⅛-inch strips (about 1 cup)
1 cup (4 ounces) frozen cut green beans or asparagus
1 package (6 ounces) frozen Chinese pea pods
3 green onions, cut diagonally in ½-inch pieces
6 tablespoons butter or margarine, cut in small pieces
6 tablespoons grated Parmesan cheese

1. Heat oven to 400°F. Have ready a baking sheet.

2. Tear off six 14x12-inch sheets of foil. Lightly spray one side of each sheet with no-stick vegetable spray or brush lightly with oil.

3. Remove the tough white ligament from the underside of each chicken-breast half by scraping along the ligament with a sharp knife. Put chicken on a cutting board and press with palms of hands to flatten evenly.

4. Place a chicken-breast half in center of lower half of each piece of foil and season each with salt and pepper. Top each with some of the bell-pepper strips, green beans, pea pods and green onions. Dot with the butter and sprinkle with the cheese.

5. Fold top half of foil over food, bringing side edges of foil together. Turn bottom edge up to meet top edge and make a double fold. Smooth with fingers. Double-fold each side securely. Arrange packets on baking sheet.

6. Bake 18 to 20 minutes, until packets are puffed and chicken is cooked through (see Is It Ready?, page 71).

7. To open packets, cut a crisscross through top of foil and turn cut ends back. Remove chicken from packets and serve.

Makes 6 servings. Per serving: 335 calories, 39 grams protein, 5 grams carbohydrate, 17 grams fat, 131 milligrams cholesterol with butter, 95 milligrams cholesterol with margarine, 344 milligrams sodium

Chicken-in-a-Packet

4 tablespoons butter or margarine
3 cups herb-seasoned stuffing mix
½ cup water
1 broiler-fryer chicken (about 2½ to
    3 pounds), quartered
Paprika
1 medium-size Golden Delicious apple,
    quartered and cored

1. Heat oven to 450°F. Have ready a baking sheet.

2. Tear off four 12-inch lengths of 18-inch-wide heavy-duty foil. Fold each sheet in half cross-wise. Lightly spray top sides of foil with no-stick vegetable spray or brush with oil.

3. Put 1 tablespoon of the butter in the center of each piece of foil. Top butter with ¾ cup of the stuffing mix and sprinkle with 2 tablespoons water. Put a piece of chicken on stuffing. Sprinkle chicken with paprika and tuck an apple wedge alongside. Fold foil closed, folding and pinching edges to seal.

4. Arrange packets on baking sheet.

5. Bake 35 minutes, until packets are puffed and chicken is cooked through (see Is It Ready?, page 71).

6. To open packets, cut a crisscross through top of foil and turn cut ends back. Remove chicken from packets and serve.

Makes 4 servings. Per serving: 671 calories, 50 grams protein, 48 grams carbohydrate, 30 grams fat, 268 milligrams cholesterol with butter, 232 milligrams cholesterol with margarine, 950 milligrams sodium

Chicken-in-a-Packet

Hobo-Style Chicken Pilaf

Hobo-Style Chicken Pilaf

Cleanup is at a minimum with this recipe because all the ingredients are assembled and baked in an oven cooking bag. For best results, use only bags made specifically for oven cooking, not food-storage or boil-in bags. To test for doneness, insert a small knife through one of the slits you've cut in the bag to see if chicken is cooked through.

  1 **tablespoon all-purpose flour**
1¾ **cups water**
  1 **cup uncooked converted long-grain**
      white rice
 ½ **cup frozen or fresh chopped onion**
 ½ **cup frozen or fresh chopped bell**
      pepper
 ½ **teaspoon salt**
 ¼ **teaspoon pepper**
  1 **broiler-fryer chicken (about**
      3 pounds), quartered
Paprika
Four 3-inch sprigs fresh thyme or
      1 teaspoon dried thyme leaves,
      crumbled
  4 **ounces fully cooked smoked**
      sausage links, cut in 1-inch
      pieces

1. Heat oven to 325°F. Put flour in a 20x14-inch oven cooking bag. Shake to coat bag with flour. Place bag in a 13x9-inch baking dish.

2. Roll down top of bag and add water, rice, onion, bell pepper, salt and pepper. Holding top of bag in one hand, gently squeeze bottom of bag with other hand to blend mixture.

3. Season chicken with paprika and, if using, dried thyme.

4. Arrange chicken in bag skin-side up on top of rice mixture. Put a fresh thyme sprig, if using, on each piece. Scatter sausage around chicken. Close bag with the nylon tie provided. Make six ½-inch slits in top.

5. Bake 1 hour, until rice and chicken are tender and liquid is absorbed. To serve, carefully cut open top of bag. Remove chicken-and-rice mixture with a large spoon to plates.

Makes 4 servings. Per serving: 408 calories, 29 grams protein, 42 grams carbohydrate, 12 grams fat, 94 milligrams cholesterol, 605 milligrams sodium

74

Relax While It Bakes

Chicken-Potato Bake

Adding a few slices of the onion to the oil while browning the chicken cuts down on spattering. Serve with a green-bean–and–shredded-carrot salad.

6 tablespoons all-purpose flour
½ teaspoon salt
¼ teaspoon pepper
1 broiler-fryer chicken (about
    3 pounds), cut up
2 tablespoons vegetable oil
4 medium-size potatoes, scrubbed and
    cut in quarters
1 large onion, sliced (about 1 cup)
1 can (14½ ounces) stewed tomatoes,
    broken up
½ cup water
1 tablespoon soy sauce

1. Heat oven to 325°F. Have ready a 13x9-inch baking pan.

2. Put flour, salt and pepper in a plastic or paper bag and shake well to mix. Add a few pieces of chicken at a time to the seasoned flour and shake until coated. Reserve remaining seasoned flour.

3. Heat oil in a large skillet over medium-high heat. Add chicken and cook about 3 minutes per side, until browned.

4. Arrange browned chicken in baking pan. Surround with potatoes and onion.

5. Discard the fat from skillet. Stir in tomatoes and reduce heat to medium.

6. Mix the reserved seasoned flour with the water in a small bowl until smooth; stir into tomatoes. Cook, stirring constantly, until thickened. Stir in soy sauce. Pour mixture over chicken, potatoes and onion.

7. Cover tightly with a lid or foil and bake 1 hour, until chicken and potatoes are fork-tender. Transfer to a heated platter and serve.

Makes 4 servings. Per serving: 494 calories, 48 grams protein, 32 grams carbohydrate, 19 grams fat, 196 milligrams cholesterol, 741 milligrams sodium

Baked Chicken—Spring Vegetable Dinner

A complete meal, made in just one pan. Serve with garlic bread or sesame bread sticks. Complete your meal with chunks of melon tossed with red or green seedless grapes.

1 large clove garlic, cut in slivers
2½ pounds chicken drumsticks
    and thighs
1 teaspoon salt
¼ teaspoon pepper
4 thin, medium-size carrots, halved
    crosswise
2 medium-size yellow summer
    squash, cut in 1-inch slices
¾ cup chicken broth
4 ounces snow-peas, trimmed
¼ cup chopped green onions

1. Heat oven to 425°F. Have ready a 13x9x2-inch shallow baking pan.

2. Tuck a sliver of garlic under the skin of each piece of chicken. Season chicken with salt and pepper and arrange skin-side up in baking pan. Bake 15 minutes.

3. Add carrots, squash and ½ cup of the broth to baking pan. Bake 25 minutes.

4. Add remaining ¼ cup broth, the snow-peas and green onions. Bake 5 minutes longer, until chicken is fork-tender and no longer pink in the center. Transfer to a heated platter and serve.

Makes 4 servings. Per serving: 407 calories, 49 grams protein, 13 grams carbohydrate, 17 grams fat, 140 milligrams cholesterol, 859 milligrams sodium

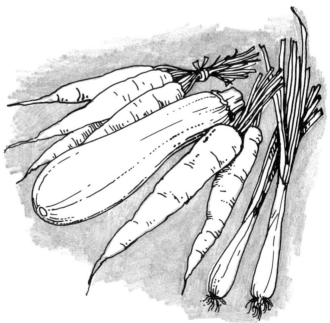

Herbed Chicken with Zucchini and Potatoes

This dish can be assembled in 15 minutes, then you can relax while it bakes. Serve with a green salad or crisp cole slaw, and ice cream for dessert.

     2 tablespoons butter or margarine
     2 tablespoons vegetable oil
     2 large cloves garlic, crushed
  1½ teaspoons dried thyme leaves
  1½ teaspoons salt
  Dash hot-pepper sauce
     1 broiler-fryer chicken (2½ to
          3 pounds), quartered
     4 small zucchini (about 1 pound),
          each scored crosswise ¼-inch
          deep along one side 3 to 4 times
     2 large russet potatoes (8 ounces
          each), halved lengthwise

1. Heat oven to 400°F.

2. Put butter, oil, garlic, thyme, salt and hot-pepper sauce in a large roasting pan or on a large ovenproof platter. Put pan in oven about 5 minutes. When butter is melted, stir to blend with other ingredients in pan.

3. Put chicken in pan and turn to coat with butter mixture. Arrange skin-side up in middle of pan. Arrange zucchini scored-side up and potatoes cut-side up around chicken. Brush with butter mixture.

4. Bake 50 minutes, until chicken is fork-tender and no longer pink in the center. Serve from pan or transfer to plates.

Makes 4 servings. Per serving: 550 calories, 47 grams protein, 23 grams carbohydrate, 30 grams fat, 249 milligrams cholesterol with butter, 231 milligrams cholesterol with margarine, 984 milligrams sodium

Herbed Chicken with Zucchini and Potatoes

Pollo Bono

Baked breaded chicken breasts topped with fresh tomatoes, onions and garlic, good with pasta and steamed vegetables. This dish is named for its originator, Sonny Bono.

Tomato Sauce
- 1 cup tomato juice
- ⅓ cup olive oil
- 2 tablespoons chopped fresh basil leaves or 2 teaspoons dried
- 2 teaspoons chopped fresh oregano leaves or ½ teaspoon dried
- 2 teaspoons minced fresh garlic
- 2 teaspoons chopped shallot
- ½ teaspoon salt
- ¼ teaspoon pepper

Chicken
- 6 boned and skinned chicken-breast halves (about 8 ounces each)
- 1 tablespoon olive oil
- ½ cup packaged seasoned dry bread crumbs
- ¼ cup grated Parmesan cheese
- 2 medium-size fresh tomatoes, each sliced in 6 rounds
- 1 medium-size onion, sliced in 12 thin rounds

1. Mix all Tomato Sauce ingredients in a medium-size saucepan (not uncoated aluminum). Bring to a boil over high heat. Reduce heat to low and simmer 5 to 7 minutes, until sauce thickens.

2. Heat oven to 375°F. Have ready a 13x9-inch broiler-proof baking dish.

3. To prepare chicken: Put chicken-breast halves in a plastic food bag. Pour in oil. Close bag and press to coat chicken with oil.

4. Mix bread crumbs and cheese on a sheet of waxed paper. Coat chicken in crumb mixture.

5. Arrange in a single layer in baking dish. Top each breast half with 2 slices each tomato and onion. Pour Tomato Sauce evenly over all.

6. Bake 30 to 35 minutes, until chicken is no longer pink in the center.

7. Turn oven selector to broil. Broil chicken 4 to 5 inches from heat source 4 to 5 minutes, until onion is tender. Transfer to a heated platter and serve.

Makes 6 servings. Per serving: 410 calories, 56 grams protein, 12 grams carbohydrate, 14 grams fat, 135 milligrams cholesterol, 808 milligrams sodium

---

✳ MICROWAVE
Chicken Casserole with Prunes

A casserole is a cook's godsend. Just assemble, put it in the oven and forget about it for two hours. Serve this soothing dish with rice, noodles or crusty bread to soak up the sauce.

- 3 large onions, sliced (about 3 cups)
- 1 tablespoon vegetable oil
- 2 tablespoons all-purpose flour
- 2 broiler-fryer chickens (about 2½ pounds each), cut up and skinned
- 2 teaspoons salt
- ½ teaspoon pepper
- 1 package (16 ounces) pitted prunes
- 1 can (15 ounces) tomato sauce

1. Heat oven to 350°F. Have ready a 4-quart casserole.

2. Put onions in casserole, drizzle with oil and sprinkle with flour. Arrange half the chicken on top; season with half the salt and pepper, then sprinkle with half the prunes. Pour half the tomato sauce over all. Repeat layers with remaining ingredients.

3. Cover casserole and bake 2 hours, until chicken is fork-tender. Serve from casserole.

Makes 8 servings. Per serving: 499 calories, 46 grams protein, 62 grams carbohydrate, 9 grams fat, 120 milligrams cholesterol, 1,049 milligrams sodium

Microwave Method: Pour half the tomato sauce over bottom of a 4-quart microwave-safe casserole. Top with half the onions, then half the chicken, with thicker portions toward outer edge of casserole. Omit the oil. Arrange half the prunes in center (they tend to overcook and possibly burn if placed near edge of casserole). Sprinkle with the flour. Repeat layers, ending with 2 additional tablespoons flour and the salt and pepper. Cover with a lid or vented plastic wrap and microwave on high 10 minutes. Rearrange chicken, bringing pieces near center to edge of casserole and keeping prunes in center. (Layers will be disturbed, but don't worry.) Spoon sauce from bottom of casserole over chicken. Cover and microwave on medium-high 30 to 35 minutes, turning chicken and spooning sauce over it after 20 minutes. Let stand directly on heat-proof countertop 10 minutes, until chicken is very tender.

Baked in Phyllo

Phyllo (or filo) pastry, a paper-thin pastry used for strudels and savory dishes, is available in most supermarket freezer or refrigerator sections. If frozen, put it in the refrigerator the night before to thaw. Phyllo looks fancy, but it's really very easy to use. And the pastry is so crunchy and crispy that everybody loves it.

Chicken-Broccoli Triangles

Serve these pastries with a salad of crisp greens, sliced beets, tomato wedges, sliced cucumber and ripe olives tossed with an olive oil—and—vinegar dressing and seasoned with a pinch of dried oregano.

4	large eggs
1½	cups cottage cheese
2	cans (5 ounces each) chunk white chicken, drained
2	packages (10 ounces each) frozen chopped broccoli, thawed and squeezed dry
½	teaspoon salt
½	teaspoon ground allspice
¼	teaspoon pepper
12	sheets (half a 1-pound package) phyllo pastry, thawed if frozen
6	tablespoons butter or margarine, melted

1. Beat eggs in a large bowl. Stir in cottage cheese, chicken, broccoli, salt, allspice and pepper until blended. Cover and chill at least 30 minutes.

2. Heat oven to 350°F. Grease two baking sheets.

3. Place one sheet phyllo on work surface with a short edge toward you (cover the remaining phyllo with plastic wrap or a sheet of waxed paper, then a lightly dampened towel). Brush with butter and top with two more sheets, buttering each. Cut sheets in half lengthwise.

4. Spoon ¼ cup of the chicken mixture about 4 inches from bottom of one strip.

5. Fold one corner of phyllo over filling to form a triangle. Continue folding triangle over and over to end of strip. Repeat with other strip and with remaining sheets of phyllo and chicken mixture until you have 8 triangles. Put triangles on prepared baking sheets and brush with butter.

6. Bake 25 minutes, until golden and flaky. Transfer to a heated platter and serve.

Makes 4 servings of 2 triangles each. Per serving: 560 calories, 40 grams protein, 30 grams carbohydrate, 27 grams fat, 382 milligrams cholesterol with butter, 328 milligrams cholesterol with margarine, 977 milligrams sodium

Chicken-Broccoli Triangles

Chicken-Phyllo Pie

This pie serves twelve, so it is a good choice for a party or a potluck supper. You can assemble this dish and keep it refrigerated up to one day before baking and serving.

Basic Poached Chicken and Broth
3 whole chicken breasts (about 4 pounds)
4 cups water
2 cups dry white wine or additional water
2 bay leaves
1 teaspoon dried rosemary leaves
1 teaspoon dried thyme leaves
2 teaspoons salt

Rice
2 tablespoons butter or margarine
1 cup chopped onion
1 teaspoon minced fresh garlic
8 ounces mushrooms, sliced
¾ cup uncooked converted white rice
1½ cups reserved chicken-poaching broth
1 package (9 ounces) frozen artichoke hearts, partially thawed and separated

Sauce
¼ cup butter or margarine
¼ cup plus 1 tablespoon all-purpose flour
2 cups reserved chicken-poaching broth
½ cup half-and-half
Pepper to taste

Phyllo Pastry
12 sheets (half a 1-pound package) phyllo dough, thawed if frozen
½ cup butter or margarine, melted

1. To poach chicken: Put chicken breasts in a large pot. Add water, wine, bay leaves, rosemary, thyme and salt. Cover and bring to a boil over high heat. Reduce heat to low and simmer 15 minutes. Remove from heat and let chicken cool in broth.

2. When chicken is cool enough to handle, discard skin and bones. Cut meat in large bite-size pieces and put in a medium-size bowl. Strain and reserve broth.

3. To make rice: Melt butter in a medium-size saucepan over medium heat. Add onion, garlic and mushrooms. Cook 3 to 5 minutes, stirring once or twice, until onion and mushrooms begin to soften.

4. Add rice and cook 3 minutes, stirring constantly. Stir in broth. Cover, raise heat to high and bring to a boil. Reduce heat to low and simmer 15 minutes.

5. Stir in artichokes and cook 5 to 10 minutes longer, until rice is tender.

6. To make sauce: Melt butter in a medium-size saucepan over low heat. Add flour and stir constantly until smooth and frothy. Let mixture bubble about 3 minutes, stirring often to prevent browning.

7. Gradually stir in broth. Increase heat to medium and simmer 5 to 7 minutes, stirring constantly, until thickened. Stir in half-and-half and simmer 3 to 4 minutes. Season with pepper.

8. Mix half the sauce with the chicken. Stir remaining sauce into the rice mixture.

9. To assemble and bake: Heat oven to 375°F, if baking right away. Lightly grease a 13x9-inch baking dish.

10. Unfold phyllo. To keep dough from drying out when not actually working with it, cover with plastic wrap or a sheet of waxed paper, then a lightly dampened towel.

11. Put one sheet phyllo in prepared dish. (As long as dough roughly fits bottom of dish, don't worry about wrinkles or edges that come slightly up the sides. If dough tears, just pat it back in place.) Brush pastry all over with melted butter. Working with one sheet at a time, layer five more sheets of dough, brushing each with butter.

12. Spread half the rice mixture over the dough. Top with the chicken mixture, then the remaining rice mixture.

13. Cover with remaining phyllo sheets, brushing each with melted butter. Tuck edges down. (At this point, the dish can be covered and refrigerated up to 24 hours.)

14. Bake 35 to 40 minutes, until golden brown. Let stand 15 minutes. Cut in squares and serve.

Makes 12 servings. Per serving (with wine): 332 calories, 20 grams protein, 16 grams carbohydrate, 16 grams fat, 87 milligrams cholesterol with butter, 45 milligrams cholesterol with margarine, 779 milligrams sodium

Oven-Fried Chicken

Oven-frying is a shortcut to crispy chicken. It eliminates the calories and the mess of deep-frying, too.

♥ **LOW-CALORIE**

Oven-Fried Almond Chicken with Cream Gravy

To remove chicken skin easily, grab it with a paper towel and pull it away along with any underlying fat.

- 1 **broiler-fryer chicken (about 3 pounds), cut up, wings and skin removed**
- 1 **tablespoon soy sauce**
- ¾ **cup packaged seasoned dry bread crumbs**
- ¼ **cup finely chopped almonds**
- ¼ **teaspoon garlic powder**
- ⅛ **teaspoon pepper**
- 1 **white from a large egg**
- 2 **teaspoons water**
- 1 **tablespoon vegetable oil**
- ¼ **teaspoon paprika**

Cream Gravy (recipe follows)

1. Heat oven to 350°F. Have ready a baking sheet.

2. Brush chicken with soy sauce.

3. Mix bread crumbs, almonds, garlic powder and pepper on a sheet of waxed paper. Lightly beat egg white and water in a shallow pie plate.

4. Dip chicken pieces in egg-white mixture, then coat with crumb mixture, gently pressing crumbs onto surface.

5. Arrange in a single layer on baking sheet. Sprinkle evenly with oil and paprika.

6. Bake 1 hour, until chicken is fork-tender and no longer pink near the bone. Serve with Cream Gravy.

Makes 4 servings. Per serving with ¼ cup gravy: 394 calories, 42 grams protein, 22 grams carbohydrate, 15 grams fat, 95 milligrams cholesterol, 860 milligrams sodium

Cream Gravy

- ¾ **cup evaporated skimmed milk**
- 1½ **tablespoons all-purpose flour**
- 1 **tablespoon dry sherry or water**
- ¾ **cup chicken broth**
- ½ **chicken-bouillon cube, crumbled**
- 1 **teaspoon chopped fresh parsley**
- ¾ **teaspoon Worcestershire sauce**

Pepper to taste

1. Whisk milk, flour and sherry in a heavy medium-size saucepan. Stir over medium heat until mixture begins to thicken and bubble. Simmer 2 minutes, stirring constantly.

2. Add remaining ingredients to saucepan. Stir well and bring to a boil. Reduce heat to low and simmer 3 to 4 minutes, stirring constantly, until gravy is thickened and smooth. Serve with the chicken.

Makes 1 cup.

Oven-Fried Chicken Thighs with Herbed Vegetables

Use the leftover evaporated milk in mashed potatoes or a pudding. Removing the skin from chicken thighs will cut calories and fat.

- 1 **cup instant mashed-potato flakes**
- 1 **teaspoon salt**
- 1 **teaspoon paprika**
- 2 **pounds chicken thighs, skinned if desired**
- ⅓ **cup evaporated milk**
- 1 **package (10 ounces) frozen mixed peas and carrots**
- 1 **cup frozen pearl onions**
- ½ **teaspoon dried thyme leaves**
- 2 **tablespoons butter or margarine**

1. Heat oven to 425°F. Have ready a 13x9-inch baking pan.

2. Mix potato flakes, ½ teaspoon of the salt and the paprika in a shallow dish.

3. Dip chicken in evaporated milk, then coat with potato mixture, pressing mixture firmly onto surface.

4. Arrange chicken skin-side up in baking pan.

5. Bake 25 minutes. Push chicken to one end of pan.

6. Meanwhile, put vegetables in a strainer. Rinse under cold running water to thaw partially. Drain vegetables.

7. Add vegetables to baking pan. Sprinkle with remaining ½ teaspoon salt and the thyme. Dot with butter. Cover only the vegetables with foil.

8. Bake 20 minutes, stirring vegetables once, until chicken and vegetables are tender. Transfer to a heated platter and serve.

Makes 4 servings. Per serving: 507 calories, 40 grams protein, 23 grams carbohydrate, 20 grams fat, 196 milligrams cholesterol with butter, 178 milligrams cholesterol with margarine, 869 milligrams sodium

Oat-Crunch Baked Chicken

Oat-Crunch Baked Chicken

For an easy go-with, scrub russet potatoes and slice in wedges. Arrange in a baking pan, drizzle with olive oil and season with salt, pepper and dried rosemary leaves. Bake in oven with the chicken. If you like, you may substitute oat bran for the oats used in this recipe; there is no need to grind the oat bran to crumbs—simply mix with the seasonings in the plastic bag.

1 **cup quick-cooking oats**
2 **teaspoons paprika**
1 **teaspoon salt**
1 **teaspoon onion powder**
⅛ **teaspoon pepper**
¼ **cup milk**
1 **broiler-fryer chicken (about
      3 pounds), cut up**
3 **tablespoons vegetable oil**

1. Heat oven to 375°F. Generously oil a shallow baking pan.

2. Put oats in a blender or a food processor and process to fine crumbs. Pour into a double plastic food bag. Add paprika, salt, onion powder and pepper. Shake well to mix.

3. Pour milk into a shallow bowl. Dip chicken in milk, then put in plastic bag with oat mixture. Shake until well coated.

4. Arrange chicken in prepared pan and drizzle with oil.

5. Bake 45 minutes, until chicken is golden brown and fork-tender. Serve on a heated platter.

Makes 4 servings. Per serving: 464 calories, 46 grams protein, 14 grams carbohydrate, 24 grams fat, 198 milligrams cholesterol, 541 milligrams sodium

Starting with Cooked

★ SPECIAL—AND WORTH IT

Chicken with Tomatillo Salsa Verde in Soft Tacos

Not all Mexican salsas are red and hot, nor are tacos always fried crisp. Originally tacos were simply fresh tortillas wrapped around a wide variety of ingredients. Make this dish for a party or a big family gathering.

¾ cup vegetable oil
Twenty-four 7-inch flour or corn tortillas
Tomatillo Salsa Verde (recipe follows)
  6 cups shredded Poached Chicken
    (recipe follows)
  1 cup shredded Monterey Jack
    cheese (4 ounces)
1½ cups sour cream
For garnish: sliced pimiento-stuffed
    green olives, Pico de Gallo (recipe
    follows) or other salsas and relishes

1. Heat oven to 200°F. Have ready one or two large, shallow baking dishes.

2. Heat about ¼ inch of the oil in a heavy medium-size skillet over medium heat.

3. For each taco, heat a tortilla in the hot oil for a few seconds just to soften. Remove with tongs, letting oil run off. Dip immediately in warm Tomatillo Salsa Verde to coat and put on a plate. Spoon about ¼ cup of the chicken down center. Top with a small amount of salsa. Roll up immediately. Arrange side by side in baking dish. When several are rolled, place in oven with door ajar. Continue filling, rolling and adding to baking dish until all tacos are filled.

4. Spoon some of the remaining salsa over tacos but do not cover completely. Sprinkle with cheese and cover with foil.

5. Increase oven temperature to 300°F. Bake tacos 5 to 10 minutes, just until cheese starts to melt.

6. Top tacos with sour cream. Garnish with olives. Serve with Pico de Gallo or other salsas and relishes.

Makes 24. Per taco (without Salsa Verde or garnish): 204 calories, 14 grams protein, 16 grams carbohydrate, 9 grams fat, 41 milligrams cholesterol, 98 milligrams sodium

Poached Chicken

2 broiler-fryer chickens (about
    3 pounds each), cut up
1 large onion, halved
4 large cloves garlic
2 stalks celery with leaves,
    cut in chunks
2 bay leaves
1 tablespoon salt
Water
Dash hot-pepper sauce (optional)

1. Put chicken, onion, garlic, celery, bay leaves and salt in a large pot. Add water to just cover chicken. Cover and bring to a boil over high heat.

2. Reduce heat to low and simmer 20 to 30 minutes, until chicken is very tender.

3. Let chicken cool in broth about 20 minutes. Remove from broth. (Strain and reserve broth for Tomatillo Salsa Verde and other uses.)

4. Remove skin from chicken and pull meat from bones. Shred meat or cut in pieces. Season with hot-pepper sauce, if desired.

Makes about 6 cups shredded chicken, 4 cups broth.

Tomatillo Salsa Verde

3 cans (10 to 13 ounces each)
    tomatillos, well drained and rinsed
¼ cup chicken broth (reserved from
    Poached Chicken)
½ cup chopped onion
1 teaspoon chopped fresh garlic
1 teaspoon salt
¼ teaspoon granulated sugar
2 sprigs fresh cilantro or ¼ teaspoon
    ground coriander
1 minced jalapeño pepper or
    1 teaspoon hot jalapeño relish
    (optional)
¼ cup vegetable oil

1. Process all ingredients except oil in a blender or a food processor until smooth.

2. Heat oil in a heavy medium-size skillet over medium-high heat. Add salsa and cook briskly 1 minute (take care—sauce may splatter). Reduce heat and simmer about 5 minutes, until sauce is slightly reduced.

Makes 4 cups. (Nutritional data unavailable.)

Pico de Gallo

6 large, firm, ripe fresh tomatoes,
    peeled, if desired, and chopped
1 large onion, finely chopped
5 green chiles, seeded and chopped, or
    2 cans (3 ounces each) whole
    peeled chiles, drained and chopped
6 sprigs fresh cilantro, finely chopped,
    or 6 sprigs Italian parsley, chopped,
    plus ½ teaspoon ground coriander
    seed
1 tablespoon fresh-squeezed lime juice,
    or to taste
1 tablespoon olive oil (optional)

Mix all ingredients in a medium-size bowl. Cover and chill before serving.

Makes 4 cups. Per ¼ cup (without oil): 22 calories, 1 gram protein, 5 grams carbohydrate, 0 grams fat, 0 milligrams cholesterol, 3 milligrams sodium

♥ LOW-CALORIE
Impossible Chicken Pie

2 cups cut-up cooked chicken or
    turkey (8 ounces)
1 jar (4½ ounces) sliced mushrooms,
    drained
½ cup sliced green onions
1 cup shredded Swiss cheese
    (4 ounces)
½ teaspoon salt
3 large eggs
¾ cup buttermilk baking mix
1½ cups milk

1. Heat oven to 400°F. Lightly grease a 10-inch pie plate.

2. Sprinkle chicken, then mushrooms, green onions, cheese and salt into pie plate.

3. Put remaining ingredients in a food processor or a blender and process 15 seconds, until smooth. Pour evenly into pie plate.

4. Bake 30 to 35 minutes, until pie is golden brown and a knife inserted halfway between center and edge comes out clean. Let stand 5 minutes. Cut in wedges and serve.

Makes 8 servings. Per serving: 224 calories, 18 grams protein, 12 grams carbohydrate, 11 grams fat, 141 milligrams cholesterol, 473 milligrams sodium

Chicken Enchiladas

Add a cooling dessert of chilled fresh pineapple chunks dusted lightly with sugar and cinnamon.

1 small clove garlic, quartered
1 can (14½ ounces) tomatoes,
    undrained
½ teaspoon dried oregano leaves
¼ teaspoon ground cumin
2 tablespoons olive oil
2½ cups shredded cooked chicken
Eight 8-inch flour tortillas
¾ cup shredded Monterey Jack or
    Cheddar cheese

1. Heat oven to 350°F. Lightly grease a 12x7-inch shallow baking dish.

2. Process garlic, tomatoes, oregano and cumin in a blender or a food processor until smooth.

3. Heat oil in a medium-size skillet over medium-high heat. Pour in tomato mixture and boil rapidly 4 minutes. Remove from heat.

4. Put chicken in a medium-size bowl and stir in ½ cup of the sauce.

5. To make enchiladas: Soften one tortilla at a time in hot sauce, turning once to coat. Lift from sauce with tongs, allowing excess sauce to run off. Put tortilla on a plate. Spoon a scant ⅓-cup chicken mixture down the center of tortilla. Fold ends over toward center and roll tortilla loosely. Put seam-side down in prepared baking dish. Repeat with remaining tortillas and chicken mixture.

6. Spread remaining sauce over the enchiladas. Sprinkle with cheese. Bake 20 minutes, until cheese melts and enchiladas are hot. Serve from baking dish.

Makes 4 servings. Per serving: 489 calories, 35 grams protein, 40 grams carbohydrate, 21 grams fat, 87 milligrams cholesterol, 339 milligrams sodium

The Busy Person's Thanksgiving

Favorite recipes with make-ahead tips for a hassle-free holiday.

Roast Turkey with Giblet Gravy

When buying a whole turkey, figure about 1 pound per serving. Because body shapes differ, cooking times can only be approximate. Cook about 15 minutes per pound for a stuffed bird up to 16 pounds. Add 12 minutes for each pound over 16. Plan to have turkey done 30 minutes before the rest of the meal. (Once cooked, a whole turkey will stay warm for at least 1 hour.)

1 turkey, thawed if frozen
Salt
Pepper
Oat, Sausage and Onion Stuffing
      (recipe follows)
Vegetable oil
Paprika (optional)
1 cup chicken broth
Giblet Gravy (recipe follows)

1. Heat oven to 325°F. Have ready a large shallow roasting pan with a rack.

2. Remove giblets, neck and any fat from turkey body or neck cavities. Discard fat. Rinse turkey and dry inside and out with paper towels. Sprinkle cavities with salt and pepper.

3. Loosely spoon Oat, Sausage and Onion Stuffing into neck cavity. Fold skin flap under back and fasten with skewers. Loosely stuff body cavity and skewer closed with lacers or trussing needle. Tie or clamp legs together. Tuck wing tips under back. Rub skin with oil, salt and pepper or paprika.

4. Place turkey breast-side up on rack in roasting pan. Insert a meat thermometer in center of thigh next to body (not touching bone). Pour chicken broth into pan. Roast, following roasting guidelines above, basting bird every 30 to 40 minutes with pan juices. Add more broth or water if pan seems dry. If breast starts to get too brown, cover loosely with a foil tent.

5. Two thirds through roasting time, untie drumsticks so that heat can penetrate cavity.

6. About 1 hour before turkey should be done, start checking meat thermometer for doneness. When thermometer in thigh reads 180° to 185°F

and center of stuffing registers 165°F (to check stuffing, insert thermometer through body cavity and leave 5 minutes), remove turkey to a platter or a carving board. (Reserve roasting pan with its drippings for Giblet Gravy.) For juice retention and easier slicing, let stand at least 30 minutes before carving. Carve and serve with stuffing and Giblet Gravy.

Per 4-ounce serving (without stuffing and gravy): 298 calories, 30 grams protein, 0 grams carbohydrate, 17 grams fat, 85 milligrams cholesterol, 213 milligrams sodium

Giblet Gravy

3 tablespoons all-purpose flour
3 cups Giblet Broth (recipe follows) plus
      reserved giblets and neck meat from
      broth
Salt and pepper to taste

1. Drain off all but 3 tablespoons drippings from roasting pan. Sprinkle with flour. Stir over medium-low heat, stirring to scrape up browned bits from bottom of pan, until mixture is golden. Remove from heat.

2. Slowly stir in Giblet Broth until blended. Stir in reserved giblets and neck meat. Bring to a boil over medium heat. Reduce heat to low and simmer 5 minutes, until thickened. Season with salt and pepper. Serve with the turkey.

Makes 3 cups. (Nutritional data unavailable.)

Giblet Broth

Turkey neck and giblets
3 cups chicken broth
1 large onion, sliced
½ cup sliced carrot
½ cup dry white wine or water
¼ cup celery leaves

1. Refrigerate liver until needed. Cut turkey neck and heart in half. Put in a medium-size saucepan along with gizzard and remaining ingredients. Bring to a boil over high heat. Reduce heat to low and simmer gently 1½ hours.

2. Add liver and simmer 30 minutes longer, until gizzard is very tender.

3. Strain broth into a 4-cup measure, pressing vegetables to extract broth (add water if necessary to measure 3 cups). Discard vegetables.

4. Chop giblets and neck meat, reserve for gravy.

Makes 3 cups broth. (Nutritional data unavailable.)

Note: Broth can be made up to two days ahead. Refrigerate broth and giblets separately.

Oat, Sausage and Onion Stuffing

    8 cups water
    2 cups steel-cut oats (12 ounces; see
       Note)
 1½ pounds pork-sausage meat, thawed
       if frozen
    3 large onions, finely chopped (about
       3 cups)
 2½ cups (8 ounces) packaged dry
       bread crumbs
    1 cup chopped fresh parsley
    4 teaspoons dried sage leaves,
       crumbled
    1 teaspoon salt
    1 teaspoon pepper

1. Bring water to a boil in a 3-quart saucepan over high heat. Add oats, cover, reduce heat to low and simmer 15 to 20 minutes, until oats are tender. Drain in a sieve and rinse under cold water to remove excess starch. Leave in sieve to drain completely.

2. Meanwhile, crumble sausage meat into a large skillet over medium heat. Cook 6 to 8 minutes, until sausage is lightly browned. Remove with a slotted spoon to a large bowl. Drain off all but 2 tablespoons drippings from skillet.

3. Add onions to skillet and cook 7 to 9 minutes, stirring occasionally, until tender. Add to sausage. Stir in the oats, bread crumbs, parsley, sage, salt and pepper. Toss to mix well.

4. Stuff into neck and body cavities of turkey, or spoon into a 3½-quart casserole. (If baking in a casserole, cover and bake in 325° to 350°F oven 30 to 45 minutes, depending on depth of dish. Uncover and bake 30 minutes longer or until top is crisp and browned.)

Makes 12 cups, enough to stuff a 15-pound bird. Per ½ cup: 157 calories, 6 grams protein, 18 grams carbohydrate, 6 grams fat, 12 milligrams cholesterol, 343 milligrams sodium

Note: Steel-cut oats, available at health-food stores, are oat groats that have been cut in small pieces with steel blades. Cook them for breakfast too; they are a delicious change from regular oatmeal or oat bran.

⏱ MAKE-AHEAD
✳ MICROWAVE

Green-Bean Casserole

This classic favorite can be assembled (except for the crispy onion topping) up to a day in advance and refrigerated.

    1 can (10¾ ounces) condensed cream
       of mushroom soup, undiluted
  ⅔ cup milk
    2 packages (9 ounces each) frozen
       French-cut green beans, thawed
       and drained
    1 can (3 ounces) sliced mushrooms,
       drained
  ¼ teaspoon salt
  ¼ teaspoon pepper
    1 can (2.8 ounces) French-fried onions

1. Heat oven to 350°F. Have ready a shallow 1½-quart baking dish.

2. Mix mushroom soup and milk in a large bowl. Add beans, mushrooms, salt and pepper and mix well. Spoon into baking dish.

3. Bake 25 minutes.

4. Scatter onions over top. Bake 10 to 15 minutes longer, until bubbly and onions are golden and crisp.

Makes 6 servings. Per serving: 127 calories, 4 grams protein, 13 grams carbohydrate, 7 grams fat, 4 milligrams cholesterol, 572 milligrams sodium

Microwave Method: Mix ingredients as directed. Spoon into a shallow 1½-quart microwave-safe baking dish. Cover with vented plastic wrap. Microwave on high 8 to 10 minutes, turning dish ½ turn and stirring once, until hot and bubbly. Scatter onions over top. Microwave uncovered on high 1 to 2 minutes, until onions are hot. Let stand 5 minutes. (If baking dish is broiler-proof, slide it under the broiler for 1 minute to crisp the onions.)

(Preceding page) Corn Pudding; Roast Turkey with Giblet Gravy; Oat, Sausage and Onion Stuffing; Cranberry-Pineapple Relish (in miniature pumpkins); Broccoli-Cheese Casserole; Green-Bean Casserole

Broccoli-Cheese Casserole

This casserole can be assembled, wrapped and frozen up to two weeks ahead. Thaw before baking.

4 large eggs
2 pounds 1%-fat cottage cheese
6 tablespoons all-purpose flour
1 bag (20 ounces) frozen cut broccoli, thawed and drained
1 loaf (8 ounces) processed cheese spread, cut in small pieces
½ cup chopped green onions
¼ cup butter or margarine, cut in small pieces

1. Heat oven to 350°F. Have ready a shallow 2½-quart baking dish.

2. Beat eggs in a large bowl. Stir in cottage cheese and flour until smooth. Stir in remaining ingredients until evenly distributed.

3. Spread in baking dish and bake 1 hour, until set and edges are golden brown.

Makes 12 servings. Per serving: 194 calories, 17 grams protein, 9 grams carbohydrate, 10 grams fat, 98 milligrams cholesterol with butter, 86 milligrams cholesterol with margarine, 665 milligrams sodium

Cranberry-Pineapple Relish

For an unusual presentation, serve this colorful relish in scooped-out uncooked miniature pumpkins, as shown, or in halves of thick-skinned oranges. The relish can be made ahead, but don't spoon into the shells until shortly before serving.

1 bag (12 ounces) fresh or frozen cranberries
2 cans (8 ounces each) crushed pineapple in juice, drained and 2 tablespoons juice reserved
¾ cup granulated sugar
½ cup finely chopped pecans, toasted

1. Coarsely chop cranberries in a food processor or in batches in a blender using on/off motion.

2. Pour into a medium-size bowl and stir in remaining ingredients, including reserved pineapple juice.

3. Cover and chill at least 1 hour or up to 1 day.

Makes 4 cups. Per ¼ cup: 86 calories, 0 grams protein, 17 grams carbohydrate, 2 grams fat, 0 milligrams cholesterol, 1 milligram sodium

Corn Pudding

This can be assembled a day ahead, covered and refrigerated.

4 large eggs
6 tablespoons butter or margarine, melted
2 tablespoons all-purpose flour
½ teaspoon *each* onion powder and salt
¼ teaspoon *each* ground red pepper and garlic powder
1 package (10 ounces) frozen corn kernels, thawed and drained (1⅔ cups)
1 can (17 ounces) cream-style corn
1 cup heavy cream

1. Heat oven to 325°F. Grease a deep 1½-quart casserole or soufflé dish.

2. Beat eggs in a large bowl. Beat in butter, flour, onion powder, salt, red pepper and garlic powder until blended. Stir in remaining ingredients. Pour into prepared casserole.

3. Bake 1½ hours, until a knife inserted near the center comes out clean. Let stand 5 minutes before serving.

Makes 8 servings. Per serving: 299 calories, 6 grams protein, 21 grams carbohydrate, 23 grams fat, 170 milligrams cholesterol with butter, 143 milligrams cholesterol with margarine, 440 milligrams sodium

To Toast the Bird

New on the market are nonalcoholic red and white grape juices made from the same types of grapes as are fine wines. Look for Riesling and zinfandel. It's a great way for everyone—drinkers, nondrinkers, even kids—to enjoy a toast together.

Convenient Turkey Parts

You don't have to roast a big bird to take advantage of turkey's great taste and price. Buy packages—breasts, thighs, drumsticks, wings, or ground to cook in a variety of delicious ways.

★ SPECIAL—AND WORTH IT

Roast Turkey Breast with Cranberry, Rice and Walnut Stuffing

Buy some turkey necks or a wing to make broth for a gravy (recipe follows).

1 boned turkey breast with skin (about
   6 pounds), thawed if frozen
½ teaspoon salt
¼ teaspoon pepper
2 cups Cranberry, Rice and Walnut
   Stuffing (recipe follows)
3 tablespoons butter or margarine, melted
For garnish: fresh cranberries and herbs
   (thyme, sage or parsley)

1. Heat oven to 325°F. Grease a 13x9-inch baking pan.

2. Open turkey breast like a book, skin-side down. Remove tenderloin (filet) from each side of breast. Scrape out white tendon from each piece with a sharp knife. Put a tenderloin on skin at each side of turkey breast. Season with salt and pepper.

3. Put reserved 2 cups stuffing down center. Fold sides over stuffing to make a neat package. Secure with skewers if necessary, then tie with white string. Place seam-side down in prepared baking pan. Lay a piece of cheesecloth over turkey breast. Pour melted butter over cloth.

4. Roast 1 hour and 15 minutes. Remove cheesecloth. Roast 20 to 30 minutes longer, until turkey is browned and a meat thermometer inserted in thickest part registers 170° to 175°F.

5. Remove turkey breast to a heated platter. Cover loosely with foil. Let stand 30 minutes before carving. Reserve pan drippings for Cranberry Pan Gravy. Garnish platter and serve.

Makes 10 servings with leftovers. Per 4-ounce serving meat: 189 calories, 34 grams protein, 0 grams carbohydrate, 4 grams fat, 65 milligrams cholesterol with butter, 64 milligrams cholesterol with margarine, 133 milligrams sodium

Cranberry, Rice and Walnut Stuffing

1 package (6¼ ounces) quick-cooking
   long-grain-and-wild-rice mix
¼ cup butter or margarine
1 cup diced celery
1 cup chopped onion
⅔ cup coarsely chopped walnuts
1 tablespoon granulated sugar
1 cup fresh or frozen cranberries
2 large eggs, lightly beaten

1. Cook rice mix as directed on package. Transfer to a large bowl and let cool 10 minutes.

2. Melt butter in a large skillet over medium heat. Add celery, onion and walnuts. Cook about 5 minutes, stirring occasionally, until vegetables are crisp-tender. Stir in sugar and cranberries and remove from heat.

3. Add vegetable mixture and eggs to rice and mix well.

4. Set aside 2 cups stuffing for turkey breast (see Note).

5. To bake remaining stuffing: Heat oven to 375°F. Put stuffing in a greased shallow 1½-quart baking dish. Bake 25 minutes, until surface is golden brown and stuffing is hot.

Makes 7 cups. Per ½ cup: 148 calories, 3 grams protein, 13 grams carbohydrate, 9 grams fat, 52 milligrams cholesterol with butter, 30 milligrams cholesterol with margarine, 270 milligrams sodium

Note: You can also use this stuffing for a whole turkey. It makes enough for a 10- to 12-pound bird.

Roast Turkey Breast with Cranberry, Rice and Walnut Stuffing

Cranberry Pan Gravy

  2 **turkey necks or 1 turkey wing**
  5 **cups water**
  1 **medium-size onion**
Few celery leaves
  1 **teaspoon salt**
Scant ¼ teaspoon dried thyme leaves
  1 **cup thawed frozen cranberry-juice**
        concentrate
1½ **tablespoons cornstarch, stirred**
        with 1 tablespoon water

1. Put necks or wing, water, onion, celery leaves, salt and thyme in a large saucepan. Bring to a boil over high heat.

2. Skim off the foam that rises to the surface. Reduce heat to low. Cover and simmer about 1½ hours, until meat is fork-tender.

3. Strain broth, reserving 1½ cups for the gravy. Save remainder of broth and turkey meat for other use. (Broth can be prepared ahead and chilled or frozen until ready to use.)

4. To make gravy: Spoon off fat from baking pan, leaving drippings and browned bits in pan.

5. Add the 1½ cups turkey broth and cranberry-juice concentrate to baking pan. Put on range top and bring to a boil over medium heat, stirring to scrape up browned bits.

6. Stir cornstarch mixture again and stir into baking pan. Bring to a boil and boil 3 to 5 minutes, stirring constantly, until thickened and clear.

Makes about 2 cups. (Nutritional data unavailable.)

Turkey Roulades

Some of the cheese filling bakes out to form a delicious sauce. Serve with fresh green or wax beans and pasta tossed with olive oil, crushed red-pepper flakes and chopped fresh parsley. For dessert, serve melon balls or chunks drizzled with lime juice. You can stuff and coat cutlets in the morning; cover and keep refrigerated until ready to bake.

- 8 thin-sliced turkey-breast cutlets (about 4 ounces each)
- 8 ounces semisoft garlic-and-herb cheese, cut in 8 pieces
- 3 large eggs
- 2 tablespoons water
- ½ cup all-purpose flour
- ¾ cup packaged Italian-style dry bread crumbs
- ¼ cup butter or margarine, melted
- For garnish: fresh parsley sprigs

1. Grease a 13x9-inch baking dish.

2. Lay cutlets flat on work surface with narrow ends toward you. Spread a piece of cheese on each to within ¼ inch of edges. Fold up long sides about ¼ inch and press into cheese. Roll up from narrow end.

3. Beat eggs and water in a pie plate. Put flour and bread crumbs on separate sheets of waxed paper.

4. Coat each cutlet in flour, dip in egg mixture and coat in bread crumbs.

5. Arrange seam-side down in prepared baking dish. Cover and chill at least 30 minutes.

6. Heat oven to 425°F.

7. Drizzle melted butter over rolled cutlets. Bake 25 to 30 minutes, until juices run clear when meat is pierced. Transfer to a heated serving platter. Garnish with parsley and serve.

Makes 8 servings. Per serving: 390 calories, 39 grams protein, 9 grams carbohydrate, 21 grams fat, 207 milligrams cholesterol with butter, 189 milligrams cholesterol with margarine, 417 milligrams sodium

Oven-Fried Turkey with Vegetable Gravy

- 1 large onion (about 8 ounces), halved lengthwise, cut in ½-inch-thick wedges
- 3 medium-size carrots, cut in 1-inch pieces
- 3 medium-size stalks celery, cut in 1-inch pieces
- ¼ cup milk
- ½ cup packaged Italian-style dry bread crumbs
- ¾ teaspoon dried thyme leaves, crumbled
- ¾ teaspoon dried sage leaves, crumbled
- 2 turkey drumsticks (about 14 ounces each)
- 2 turkey thighs (about 12 ounces each)
- ¼ cup cider vinegar
- 1 cup chicken broth

1. Heat oven to 400°F. Have ready a large roasting pan.

2. Scatter onion, carrots and celery in bottom of roasting pan.

3. Pour milk into a pie plate or a large shallow bowl.

4. Mix bread crumbs, thyme and sage on a sheet of waxed paper.

5. Dip turkey in milk, then coat in crumb mixture. Arrange in roasting pan.

6. Roast 1½ hours, until turkey is golden and crisp and juices run clear when meat is pierced. Transfer to a heated platter; cover and keep warm.

7. Skim off and discard fat in roasting pan.

8. Place pan of vegetables on range top across two burners. Add vinegar and cook over medium-high heat, stirring to scrape up browned bits from bottom of pan. When vinegar is reduced to 2 tablespoons, add broth and bring to a boil.

9. Remove from heat and carefully ladle vegetables and broth into a food processor or a blender (in batches if necessary). Process until smooth. Serve gravy with the turkey.

Makes 4 to 6 servings. Per 4 ounces cooked turkey with ¼ cup gravy: 433 calories, 35 grams protein, 26 grams carbohydrate, 20 grams fat, 125 milligrams cholesterol, 645 milligrams sodium

Crisp Turkey Thighs with Chick-peas and Tomatoes

Remove the turkey skin by pulling it while cutting between skin and meat with a small, sharp knife. Cooked without skin, the meat has better flavor, less fat and fewer calories. Serve this dish with crisp bread sticks and sliced cucumber dressed with yogurt and crumbled dried mint.

¼ cup butter or margarine
1 large clove garlic, crushed
2 large turkey thighs (about 1 pound each), skinned
½ cup packaged seasoned dry bread crumbs
1 teaspoon dry mustard
¼ teaspoon salt
1 can (16 ounces) chick-peas, drained
1 package (9 to 10 ounces) frozen cut green beans (2 cups)
1 can (15 ounces) tomatoes, drained
For garnish: minced fresh parsley

1. Place butter and garlic in a shallow baking dish. Turn on oven to 350°F. Place dish in oven about 5 minutes, until butter melts. Remove from oven.

2. Cut turkey thighs in half lengthwise along the bone, leaving the bone in one half.

3. Mix crumbs, mustard and salt on a sheet of waxed paper. Roll turkey in melted butter, then coat in crumb mixture, pressing crumbs firmly onto turkey.

4. Put chick-peas and beans in baking dish and stir to coat with remaining garlic butter. Arrange thigh pieces on top.

5. Bake 50 minutes, until turkey is almost tender.

6. Place tomatoes between pieces of turkey and bake 10 minutes longer, until turkey is tender and tomatoes hot. Sprinkle parsley over tomatoes. Transfer to a heated platter and serve.

Makes 4 servings. Per serving: 544 calories, 43 grams protein, 37 grams carbohydrate, 24 grams fat, 151 milligrams cholesterol with butter, 115 milligrams cholesterol with margarine, 629 milligrams sodium

Crisp Turkey Thighs with Chick-peas and Tomatoes

Oven-Barbecued Turkey Wings with Szechuan Hot-and-Spicy Sauce

Oven-Barbecued Turkey Wings with Szechuan Hot-and-Spicy Sauce

Turkey wings can be purchased whole or divided. This recipe makes excellent use of the flat-wing section. If you can find only whole wings, cut through them at each joint. Freeze the tips to use for stock. You can use the drumettes (the thicker parts, closest to the body) for Wingding Gumbo with Sweet Potatoes and Red Bell Peppers (see Index). Crisp fried potatoes and a cucumber salad are nice additions to Oven-Barbecued Turkey Wings.

8 turkey flat-wing sections (about
      8 ounces each)
⅔ cup tomato ketchup
⅔ cup soy sauce
½ cup dry sherry or water
¼ cup finely chopped onion
2 tablespoons packed brown sugar
2 tablespoons hot-pepper sauce,
      or to taste
2 teaspoons minced fresh garlic
1 tablespoon minced fresh gingerroot
      or 2 teaspoons ground ginger

1. Bring a large pot of water to a boil over high heat. Add wings and return to a boil. Reduce heat to medium-low and simmer 30 minutes. Drain. (Reserve the broth for other uses.)

2. Heat oven to 350°F. Have ready a 15½x10½-inch jelly-roll pan fitted with a rack. Place wings on rack.

3. Process remaining ingredients in a food processor or a blender until smooth. Brush on both sides of wings. Arrange wings top-side up on rack, in a single layer. Bake about 1 hour, brushing once or twice with sauce, until meat is tender and skin brown and crisp. Remove to a heated platter. Put remaining sauce in a bowl and serve with wings.

Makes 4 servings. Per serving with 2 tablespoons sauce (with sherry): 431 calories, 38 grams protein, 6 grams carbohydrate, 23 grams fat, 158 milligrams cholesterol, 1,130 milligrams sodium

Braised Drumsticks with Black-eyed Peas and Turnips

⏱ MAKE-AHEAD

Braised Drumsticks with Black-eyed Peas and Turnips

Serve with hot corn bread or corn sticks.

- 1 envelope golden onion-soup mix (from a 2.6-ounce package)
- 2 cups water
- 1 rounded tablespoon prepared mustard
- 1 teaspoon dried thyme leaves
- ¼ teaspoon pepper, or to taste
- 3 pounds turkey drumsticks
- 1 package (10 ounces) frozen black-eyed peas, thawed
- 1 cup frozen small white onions, thawed
- 6 ounces mushrooms, quartered (about 2 cups)
- 2 medium-size carrots, halved lengthwise and cut in ½-inch-thick slices
- 3 medium-size white turnips (about 1 pound), halved

For garnish: parsley sprigs

1. Heat oven to 350°F.

2. Stir soup mix, water, mustard, thyme and pepper in a large roasting pan until blended. Add drumsticks and black-eyed peas.

3. Cover with foil and bake 1 hour and 15 minutes.

4. Remove from oven. Add remaining vegetables and replace foil. Bake 25 to 30 minutes longer, until vegetables are tender.

5. Transfer drumsticks to a cutting board. Cover vegetables with foil to keep warm.

6. When drumsticks are cool enough to handle, remove skin and slice meat from bone; discard tough tendons.

7. Arrange meat on a heated platter and surround with vegetables and braising liquid. Garnish with parsley and serve.

Makes 4 servings. Per serving: 545 calories, 60 grams protein, 34 grams carbohydrate, 15 grams fat, 170 milligrams cholesterol, 894 milligrams sodium

Braised Drumsticks and Vegetables in Tomato Cream

Serve with hot biscuits.

- 1 package (2.7 ounces) Swiss tomato-soup mix with basil
- 1 cup sour cream
- ½ cup dry vermouth or water
- ½ cup chicken broth or water
- ¼ teaspoon pepper, or to taste
- 3 pounds turkey drumsticks
- 1 pound small red or white thin-skinned potatoes
- 3 stalks celery, halved
- 8 small thin carrots
- 12 ounces small onions

For garnish: chopped fresh parsley

1. Heat oven to 350°F.

2. Stir soup mix, sour cream, vermouth, broth and pepper in a large roasting pan until blended. Add drumsticks to sauce.

3. Cover with foil and bake 1 hour and 15 minutes.

4. Remove from oven. Add vegetables to pan. Replace foil and bake 25 to 30 minutes longer, until meat and vegetables are tender.

5. Transfer drumsticks to a cutting board. Cover vegetables with foil to keep warm.

6. When drumsticks are cool enough to handle, remove skin and slice meat from bone; discard tough tendons.

7. Arrange meat on a heated serving platter and surround with vegetables and some of the sauce. Put remaining sauce in a gravy boat or a bowl. Sprinkle turkey and vegetables with parsley and serve.

Makes 6 servings. Per serving (with vermouth and broth): 442 calories, 39 grams protein, 29 grams carbohydrate, 18 grams fat, 133 milligrams cholesterol, 583 milligrams sodium

Braised Drumsticks and Vegetables in Tomato Cream

Turkey Torte

Serve this main-dish pie with your favorite chutney or with soy sauce and a green salad on the side.

1 can (3 ounces) chow-mein noodles
2 tablespoons butter or margarine, cut in small pieces
White from 1 large egg, beaten with fork until frothy
1 pound ground turkey
1 can (14 ounces) chop-suey vegetables, drained
1 tablespoon soy sauce
½ teaspoon garlic powder
¼ teaspoon pepper

1. Heat oven to 375°F. Have ready a nonstick 8-inch round cake pan (or line bottom of uncoated pan with waxed paper and grease paper and pan sides).

2. Crush 1 cup of the noodles with the butter in a food processor or a medium-size bowl with a pastry blender until mixture is crumbly and pasty. If using a processor, transfer mixture to a medium-size bowl. Add remaining noodles and the egg white and mix well. Press firmly into the bottom of prepared cake pan.

3. Bake 12 minutes, until crust is firm and shrinks slightly from sides. Remove from oven. Raise oven temperature to 425°F.

4. In same bowl, mix turkey, vegetables, soy sauce, garlic powder and pepper. Press firmly and evenly over baked crust and to edge of pan. (During baking, meat mixture will shrink to size of crust.)

5. Bake 20 minutes, until meat mixture feels firm and juices are clear. Invert onto an ovenproof serving plate. Drain off juices.

6. Return to oven for 3 to 5 minutes to crisp crust on top. Cut in wedges and serve.

Makes 4 servings. Per serving: 328 calories, 32 grams protein, 11 grams carbohydrate, 15 grams fat, 101 milligrams cholesterol with butter, 83 milligrams cholesterol with margarine, 699 milligrams sodium

Turkey-Sausage Loaf

1 pound ground turkey
1 pound fresh or thawed frozen turkey breakfast sausage (see Note)
1 cup coarsely shredded carrots
1 medium-size onion, chopped (about ½ cup)
1 cup fresh bread crumbs (from 2 slices white bread)
1 large egg
⅓ cup milk
¼ cup chopped fresh parsley
⅓ cup tomato ketchup
1 tablespoon packed brown sugar
½ teaspoon dry mustard

1. Heat oven to 350°F. Lightly grease a 13x9-inch baking pan.

2. Mix meats, carrots, onion, bread crumbs, egg, milk and parsley in a large bowl until well blended.

3. Put meat mixture in prepared pan and shape into loaf about 2½ inches thick. Mix remaining ingredients and spread over loaf.

4. Bake 45 minutes, until loaf is no longer pink in center. Let stand 10 minutes before slicing.

Makes 8 servings. Per serving: 344 calories, 27 grams protein, 17 grams carbohydrate, 18 grams fat, 290 milligrams cholesterol, 660 milligrams sodium

Note: If turkey sausage is unavailable, substitute 1 pound pork sausage. Cook 10 minutes longer, or until a meat thermometer inserted in center registers 170°F.

Baked Cornish Hens with Rice

★ SPECIAL—AND WORTH IT
Baked Cornish Hens with Rice

These wonderful birds are a staple in both the frozen and fresh poultry cases. Their average weight is 1½ pounds, so each one serves two. Fresh artichokes would make a lovely start to this meal; dip the leaves in lemon butter. To accompany the birds, cook thin strips of zucchini in olive oil; season with minced garlic and fresh or dried basil.

3 Cornish hens (about 1½ pounds each), thawed if frozen
2 tablespoons lemon juice
1 package (6 ounces) long-grain-and-wild-rice mix
¼ cup dry white wine (optional)
For garnish: green grapes

1. Heat oven to 450°F. Lightly grease a 13x9-inch baking pan.

2. Rub cavities of hens with lemon juice and place breast side-up in prepared pan, tucking wing tips under. Bake 15 minutes.

3. Meanwhile, cook rice mix according to package directions, but only for 15 minutes.

4. Remove hens from oven. Reduce oven temperature to 350°F.

5. Fill hen body cavities with rice mix and tie legs together. Pour wine over birds, if desired.

6. Bake 30 to 35 minutes, until hens are lightly browned, juices run clear when thigh is pierced and internal temperature registers 165° to 170°F on a meat thermometer.

7. Place hens on a heated serving platter. Garnish with grapes. Cut in half to serve.

Makes 6 servings. Per serving (without wine): 363 calories, 33 grams protein, 22 grams carbohydrate, 15 grams fat, 123 milligrams cholesterol, 595 milligrams sodium

On the Grill

There is nothing quite like the flavor and aroma of food grilled over charcoal or broiled to crisp perfection indoors. Poultry is perfect for the grill; a snappy sauce, a zesty marinade or a spicy rub just adds to the special flavor.

Sauces at top: Soy-Honey Glaze, Pesto, Butter Sauce (for Two-Sauce Chicken), Carolina Mustard Sauce.
On grill, from bottom: Two-Sauce Chicken, Carolina Mustard Chicken, Soy-Honey Glazed Chicken Breasts

Marinades and Bastes

Our grilling instructions are for cooking over charcoal. When using a gas grill, follow manufacturer's directions for using drip pans and arranging lava rocks.

Grilling Tips

☐ **How Hot?:** Start a charcoal fire 30 to 40 minutes before cooking. Here's how to determine the temperature of the fire on an open grill:

Very Hot (450°–500°F): Coals should be glowing with some gray ash around the edges.

Hot (400°–450°F): Coals are covered with gray ash; you can hold your hand over coals at cooking height for 2 to 3 seconds.

Medium (350°–400°F): You can hold your hand over coals for 4 seconds.

Low (300°–350°F): You can hold your hand over coals for 5 to 6 seconds.

To determine the heat of a closed grill, set an oven thermometer inside at cooking height.

☐ **Barbecue Safety:** Make sure your grill is located on a flat, level surface, away from overhangs and fences that could be ignited. Never use gasoline or kerosene as a fire starter, and never, never add lighter fluid directly to hot coals. Instead, to give spark to a sluggish fire, soak a few briquettes in lighter fluid in a small metal container for a few seconds, add to coals and light. Don't cover a charcoal grill until you are ready to cook. Covering the grill might put out the fire or prevent lighter fluid from being completely burned off, giving food an off taste.

☐ **The Helpful Microwave:** Cut grilling time by precooking poultry in the microwave. A 3-pound cut-up chicken will be done to golden perfection in 15 minutes over hot coals if first cooked, loosely covered, in a microwave on high for 10 minutes (rearrange chicken halfway through cooking time). For an example of this time-saving trick, see Barbecued Turkey.

☐ **Ready Yet?:** Cooking times given in recipes are approximate and should be used only as guides. Outdoor temperature, wind and type of grill all make a difference. Check food often for best results.

☐ **What's That Wonderful Smell?** Soak stalks of fresh herbs or dried aromatic herbs such as basil, thyme, tarragon or oregano in cold water for about 1 hour. Drain well, then toss herbs onto hot coals just before adding foods to be grilled. Orange or lemon peels added to the coals will also add a delicate flavor to poultry and vegetables.

Basting Directions

Mix all ingredients in a small bowl until well blended. Using a long-handled basting brush, brush foods frequently during cooking.

Chili-Apricot Baste

¾ cup tomato chili sauce
⅓ cup apricot preserves
1 tablespoon Worcestershire sauce
1 teaspoon minced fresh garlic
Makes 1 cup.

Hot and Tangy Baste

⅔ cup vegetable oil
½ cup cider vinegar
¼ cup tomato paste
1 tablespoon finely chopped onion
1 tablespoon dried basil leaves
1 tablespoon salt
1 teaspoon hot-pepper sauce,
   or to taste
Makes 1½ cups.

Orange-Ginger Baste

1 can (6 ounces) frozen orange-juice
   concentrate, thawed
¼ cup cider vinegar
1 tablespoon honey
1 tablespoon soy sauce
¾ teaspoon ground ginger
Makes 1¼ cups.

Garlic-Pepper Marinade

This recipe suggests a range for the red-pepper flakes and minced fresh garlic so that you can season to your taste.

- 1 cup olive oil
- 1½ teaspoons freshly grated lime peel
- 2 tablespoons fresh-squeezed lime juice
- 1 to 2 tablespoons crushed red-pepper flakes
- 1 to 2 tablespoons minced fresh garlic
- 3 whole black peppercorns
- 1 teaspoon whole coriander seed (optional)

Before grilling, scrape pepper flakes and garlic off food. Strain marinade and use as a baste during grilling.

Makes 1¼ cups.

Lemon-Rosemary Marinade

Especially good with thin-sliced turkey-breast cutlets or vegetables.

- 1 cup lemon juice
- ⅔ cup olive oil
- 2 tablespoons dried rosemary leaves
- ½ teaspoon salt
- ¼ teaspoon pepper

Makes 1⅔ cups.

Chile-Cumin Marinade

- 1 cup olive oil
- ½ cup red-wine vinegar
- 1 tablespoon chili powder
- 1 teaspoon ground cumin
- ½ teaspoon salt

Makes 1½ cups.

🕐 **MAKE-AHEAD**

Savory Grilled or Broiled Chicken

- ⅓ cup vegetable oil
- ¼ cup soy sauce
- ¼ cup lemon juice
- 2 tablespoons prepared mustard
- 1 teaspoon minced fresh garlic
- 1 broiler-fryer chicken (about 3 pounds), cut up

1. Mix all ingredients except chicken in a large shallow dish. Add chicken and turn to coat. Cover and refrigerate 4 hours or overnight, turning pieces once.

2. Remove chicken; reserve marinade.

3. Prepare barbecue grill or turn on broiler.

4. To grill: Grill skin-side up directly on rack 5 to 6 inches from hot coals 25 minutes, brushing chicken twice with marinade. Turn and grill 15 to 20 minutes longer, basting twice, until chicken is no longer pink near the bone and juices run clear when chicken is pierced. Arrange on a heated platter and serve.

To broil: Broil skin-side down 5 to 6 inches from heat source, following grilling directions above.

Makes 4 servings. Per serving: 463 calories, 44 grams protein, 2 grams carbohydrate, 30 grams fat, 196 milligrams cholesterol, 1,251 milligrams sodium

Chicken Thighs with Pesto

(Shown on page 98)

Pesto sauce has become a national passion; it is good on everything from pasta to fish and is absolutely scrumptious on chicken thighs. When basil is abundant, make several batches of Pesto (omitting the cheese; stir it in just before serving or using) and freeze in airtight containers with a little olive oil drizzled over the surface. The frozen sauce may darken, but the flavor will be just as delicious.

⅓ **cup vegetable oil**
⅓ **cup Pesto (recipe follows)**
12 **chicken thighs (about 3 pounds)**

1. Beat oil and pesto with a fork in a shallow baking dish until well mixed. Turn chicken in sauce to coat evenly. Cover and let stand at room temperature 30 minutes.

2. Meanwhile, prepare barbecue grill or turn oven selector to broil and temperature control to 450°F.

3. Remove chicken; reserve marinade.

4. To grill: Arrange chicken skin-side up directly on rack 3 to 4 inches above hot coals. Grill 35 minutes, turning and basting twice with marinade, until chicken is tender and no longer pink in the center.

To broil: Arrange chicken skin-side down on a lightly greased broiler-pan rack. Broil 5 to 6 inches from heat source 20 minutes per side, until skin is crisp and slightly charred, brushing with reserved marinade after 10 minutes, until chicken is done, as described above.

5. To serve, arrange chicken on a heated platter. If desired, serve with a bowl of additional pesto, at room temperature.

Makes 6 servings. Per serving (without additional pesto): 492 calories, 38 grams protein, 3 grams carbohydrate, 37 grams fat, 119 milligrams cholesterol, 219 milligrams sodium

Pesto

2 **cups loosely packed fresh basil leaves**
2 **cloves garlic, crushed**
¼ **cup walnut pieces or pine nuts**
½ **to ¾ cup olive oil**
½ **cup freshly grated Parmesan cheese**
¼ **teaspoon salt, or to taste**

1. Process basil, garlic, nuts and ½ cup oil in a food processor or a blender until almost smooth. (If sauce is pasty, add additional oil.)

2. Scrape into a small bowl and beat in cheese and salt. Taste, and add more salt if desired. Refrigerate until ready to use.

Makes about 1 cup. Per 2 tablespoons (with walnuts and ½ cup oil): 165 calories, 3 grams protein, 1 gram carbohydrate, 17 grams fat, 5 milligrams cholesterol, 111 milligrams sodium

⏱ **MAKE-AHEAD**
♥ **LOW-CALORIE**

Soy-Honey Glazed Chicken Breasts

(Shown on page 98)

The glaze adds an attractive shine and piquant flavor to the chicken.

½ **cup soy sauce**
¼ **cup minced green onions**
2 **tablespoons dry sherry**
1 **tablespoon honey**
2 **teaspoons minced fresh garlic**
2 **teaspoons grated fresh gingerroot (optional)**
4 **chicken-breast halves (about 8 ounces each), skinned**

1. Mix all ingredients except chicken in a small bowl.

2. Dip chicken in sauce, then put in a doubled plastic food bag; pour in remaining sauce. Close tight and marinate at room temperature 30 minutes to 1 hour.

3. Remove chicken; reserve sauce.

4. Prepare barbecue grill or turn on broiler.

5. To grill: Arrange chicken skinned-side up directly on rack about 4 inches above hot coals. Grill 25 minutes, turning as needed to prevent charring and brushing with reserved sauce to keep moist, until chicken is no longer pink in the center.

To broil: Arrange chicken skinned-side down on lightly greased broiler-pan rack. Broil 5 to 6 inches from heat source 30 minutes, turning once and brushing with reserved sauce as needed to keep chicken moist, until evenly browned and no longer pink in the center.

6. Arrange chicken on a heated platter. Bring any remaining sauce to a boil and serve with chicken.

Makes 4 servings. Per serving with 2 tablespoons sauce: 181 calories, 26 grams protein, 9 grams carbohydrate, 4 grams fat, 89 milligrams cholesterol, 2,722 milligrams sodium

Two-Sauce Chicken

(Shown on page 98)

To avoid charring chicken on the grill, extinguish any flames by spritzing with water.

> 2 broiler-fryer chickens (about 2½
>   pounds each), quartered

Marinade

> 1 cup cider vinegar
> 3 tablespoons lemon juice
> 1½ tablespoons tomato ketchup
> 1½ teaspoons Dijon mustard
> ½ teaspoon salt
> ¼ teaspoon pepper

Butter Sauce

> ⅓ cup butter, melted
> ¼ cup granulated sugar
> 2 tablespoons Dijon mustard
> 1 tablespoon Worcestershire sauce
> 1 teaspoon salt

1. Put chicken in a single layer in a large dish or in a doubled plastic food bag. Mix marinade ingredients in a small bowl and pour over chicken. Turn to coat with marinade. Cover dish or close bag and refrigerate overnight.

2. Mix all Butter Sauce ingredients in a bowl.

3. Prepare barbecue grill or turn oven selector to broil and temperature control to 450°F.

4. Remove chicken; reserve marinade.

5. To grill: Arrange chicken skin-side down directly on rack 4 to 6 inches above hot coals. Grill 5 minutes. Turn chicken, baste with reserved marinade and grill about 20 minutes, until chicken starts to brown. Grill chicken 30 minutes longer, basting lightly with Butter Sauce and turning once or twice, until fork-tender and no longer pink in the center.

To broil: Arrange chicken skin-side up on a lightly greased broiler-pan rack. Broil 5 to 6 inches from heat source 15 minutes, basting with marinade two or three times. Brush with Butter Sauce and broil 5 minutes. Turn chicken and repeat procedure. Turn chicken skin-side up and brush with Butter Sauce. Broil 10 minutes longer, brushing twice, until dark brown and glazed and chicken tests done, as described above.

6. To serve, arrange on a heated platter. Serve remaining Butter Sauce on the side.

Makes 8 servings. Per serving with 1½ tablespoons Butter Sauce: 276 calories, 30 grams protein, 10 grams carbohydrate, 13 grams fat, 132 milligrams cholesterol, 433 milligrams sodium

Carolina Mustard Chicken

(Shown on page 98)

Barbecue chefs seldom realize how much a good broth can enhance the flavor of the basting sauce. You don't taste the broth, but it gives the chicken a richer and deeper flavor.

> 8 meaty chicken pieces, your choice:
>   breasts, thighs, drumsticks
>   (about 2½ pounds)
> ¼ cup vegetable oil or melted butter
> 1½ cups well-seasoned chicken broth
> ¼ cup Dijon mustard

1. Brush chicken with oil. Reserve remaining oil.

2. Prepare barbecue grill or turn on broiler.

3. To grill: Arrange chicken skin-side up directly on rack about 4 inches above medium-hot coals. Grill until browned, turning and basting with oil once. Add chicken broth and mustard to reserved oil and mix well. Heat at edge of the grill. Brush chicken generously with sauce and grill 30 to 45 minutes, turning and basting with sauce as needed to cook evenly and prevent charring, until tender and no longer pink in the center.

To broil: Brush both sides of chicken with oil. Arrange skin-side down on a baking sheet. Broil about 6 inches from heat source 10 minutes, until golden. Mix chicken broth and mustard with remaining oil. Brush chicken with mustard sauce and turn skin-side up. Broil 10 minutes, brushing with sauce two or three times. Turn and broil 10 minutes longer, turning and basting each side once with sauce, until evenly browned and crisp and chicken tests done, as described above. Heat some of the remaining sauce in a small saucepan (see Note).

4. To serve, arrange chicken on a heated serving platter. Serve the mustard sauce on the side.

Makes 4 servings. Per serving with 2 tablespoons sauce: 179 calories, 33 grams protein, 0 grams carbohydrate, 5 grams fat, 126 milligrams cholesterol with oil, 162 milligrams cholesterol with butter, 242 milligrams sodium

Note: For broiled chicken, you'll need only half the amount of sauce. You can store the rest tightly covered in the refrigerator for up to two weeks.

Yogurt-Cumin Chicken and Vegetables

Yogurt-Cumin Chicken and Vegetables

4 **boned and skinned chicken-breast halves (about 4 ounces each)**
⅓ **cup plain low-fat yogurt**
3 **tablespoons apricot preserves**
1 **teaspoon ground cumin**
1 **teaspoon salt**
2 **yellow summer squash (about 5 ounces each), cut lengthwise in ¼-inch-thick slices**
2 **sweet potatoes (about 8 ounces each), cut lengthwise in ¼-inch-thick slices**
2 **tablespoons vegetable oil**
Pepper to taste
8 **medium-size green onions, ends trimmed**

1. Remove broiler pan from oven. Turn on broiler.

2. Cut three shallow slits lengthwise in skinned side of each chicken breast. Put chicken slit-side down in center of broiler-pan rack.

3. Mix yogurt, preserves, cumin and ½ teaspoon of the salt in a small bowl. Brush on chicken.

4. Arrange squash and potatoes around chicken. Brush with some of the oil and season with pepper and remaining ½ teaspoon salt.

5. Broil 3 to 4 inches from heat source 4 minutes. Turn vegetables. Add green onions to broiler-pan rack and brush all with remaining oil. Turn chicken and brush with remaining yogurt mixture. Broil 5 minutes longer, until chicken is no longer pink in the center.

Makes 4 servings. Per serving: 347 calories, 26 grams protein, 39 grams carbohydrate, 10 grams fat, 57 milligrams cholesterol, 599 milligrams sodium

Tandoori Chicken

Thinly sliced onions, lemon wedges and pita bread or *pappadum* (crisp Indian breads) are the traditional accompaniments. Serve this dish with a well-seasoned wheat pilaf and a green vegetable. This recipe weighs in at less than 300 calories per serving; to reduce fat and calories even further, remove the skin from the chicken and don't use the wings, which are almost impossible to skin.

- 1 cup plain low-fat yogurt
- ½ cup fresh-squeezed lemon juice
- 4 teaspoons ground coriander seed
- 4 teaspoons ground cumin
- 4 teaspoons salt
- 1 tablespoon minced fresh garlic
- 2 teaspoons freshly grated gingerroot (see Note) or 1 teaspoon ground ginger
- 1 teaspoon turmeric
- ¾ teaspoon ground red pepper
- 2 broiler-fryer chickens (about 3 pounds each), cut up

1. Mix yogurt, lemon juice, coriander, cumin, salt, garlic, gingerroot, turmeric and ground red pepper in a large bowl or a doubled plastic food bag. Add chicken pieces and cover bowl or close bag. Marinate in refrigerator 24 to 48 hours, turning several times.

2. Prepare barbecue grill or turn on broiler.

3. Drain chicken; discard marinade.

4. To grill: Arrange chicken directly on rack 4 to 6 inches above hot coals. Grill chicken 15 to 20 minutes per side, until no longer pink in the center.

To broil: Arrange chicken on broiler-pan rack. Broil 4 to 5 inches from heat source 15 to 20 minutes per side, until chicken tests done, as described above.

5. Arrange chicken on a heated platter and serve.

Makes 6 servings. Per serving: 290 calories, 50 grams protein, 3 grams carbohydrate, 7 grams fat, 177 milligrams cholesterol, 997 milligrams sodium

Note: To make fresh gingerroot last longer and grate more easily, wrap and freeze it unpeeled. Grate or slice gingerroot while still frozen. Rewrap and store in the freezer.

Chicken-Curry Kabobs on Rice

Serve kabobs with a crisp green salad dressed with garlic vinaigrette.

- ½ cup plain low-fat yogurt
- 1 teaspoon minced fresh garlic
- ¼ teaspoon **each** curry powder, chili powder, ground ginger and salt
- 1½ pounds boned and skinned chicken-breast halves, cut in 1-inch pieces
- Six 8- to 10-inch skewers (if bamboo, soak in water 1 hour)
- 3 cups freshly cooked long-grain white rice (yield from 1 cup uncooked)
- 1 large ripe fresh tomato (8 ounces), finely chopped (about 1 cup)
- 2 medium-size green onions, thinly sliced (about ¼ cup)
- For garnish: fresh cilantro or parsley leaves

1. Mix yogurt, garlic, curry powder, chili powder, ginger and salt in a large bowl or a doubled plastic food bag.

2. Add chicken and cover bowl or close bag. Marinate in refrigerator at least 6 hours or overnight, turning several times.

3. Prepare barbecue grill or turn on broiler.

4. Drain chicken; discard marinade.

5. Thread chicken pieces onto skewers, leaving room at one end for easy handling and leaving space between pieces for even cooking.

6. To grill: Place skewers directly on rack 4 to 6 inches above hot coals. Grill 8 to 10 minutes, turning skewers twice, until chicken feels firm and is golden and tender.

To broil: Place skewers on broiler-pan rack. Broil 4 to 5 inches from heat source 4 to 5 minutes per side, until chicken tests done, as described above.

7. To serve, toss freshly cooked rice with tomato and green onions in a medium-size bowl. Spoon rice mixture onto a heated platter. Arrange skewers of chicken on top and garnish with cilantro leaves.

Makes 6 servings. Per serving: 283 calories, 33 grams protein, 27 grams carbohydrate, 4 grams fat, 76 milligrams cholesterol, 495 milligrams sodium

Under the Broiler

Deviled Chicken with Vegetables

Good with a tossed green salad or ripe tomato wedges.

- ⅛ **teaspoon poultry seasoning**
- ¼ **cup coarse-grain mustard**
- 4 **boned and skinned chicken-breast halves (about 4 ounces each)**
- 1 **can (16 ounces) sliced white potatoes, drained**
- 1 **jar (6 ounces) quartered marinated artichoke hearts, undrained**
- 2 **medium-size zucchini (4 to 5 ounces each), sliced in ¼-inch-thick rounds**
- ¼ **cup grated Parmesan cheese**

1. Remove broiler pan from oven. Turn on broiler. Line broiler-pan rack with foil and spray foil with no-stick vegetable cooking spray.

2. Stir poultry seasoning into mustard.

3. Put chicken breasts skinned-side down, on one side of rack. Spread chicken with half the mustard mixture.

4. Toss remaining ingredients in a medium-size bowl until well coated with the artichoke marinade and cheese. Arrange next to chicken.

5. Broil 3 to 4 inches from heat source 4 minutes. Turn chicken, spread with remaining mustard mixture and broil 4 to 5 minutes longer, until chicken is no longer pink in the center and the vegetables start to brown. Transfer to a heated platter and serve.

Makes 4 servings. Per serving: 330 calories, 30 grams protein, 27 grams carbohydrate, 12 grams fat, 61 milligrams cholesterol, 308 milligrams sodium

Deviled Chicken with Vegetables

Buffalo Chicken Thighs with Broiled Potatoes and Carrot and Celery Sticks with Blue-Cheese Dressing

Buffalo Chicken Thighs with Broiled Potatoes and Carrot and Celery Sticks with Blue-Cheese Dressing

A main-course version of the popular appetizer Buffalo Chicken Wings.

- 3 **tablespoons vegetable oil**
- 1 **to 2 tablespoons hot-pepper sauce, or to taste**
- ½ **teaspoon minced fresh garlic**
- 8 **chicken thighs (about 4 ounces each)**
- 2 **large russet potatoes (about 8 ounces each), scrubbed and cut in ¼-inch-thick rounds**
- ¼ **teaspoon *each* salt and pepper**
- 2 **large carrots, peeled and cut in sticks**
- 2 **large stalks celery, cut in sticks**
- 1 **cup bottled blue-cheese dressing**

1. Remove broiler pan from oven. Line broiler-pan rack with foil and spray foil with no-stick vegetable cooking spray. Turn on broiler.

2. Put oil, hot-pepper sauce and garlic in a small bowl and whisk until blended.

3. Arrange chicken skin-side up in a single layer on center of broiler-pan rack. Brush with oil mixture.

4. Arrange potatoes in a single layer around chicken. Sprinkle with half the salt and pepper.

5. Broil chicken and potatoes 4 to 6 inches from heat source 10 to 12 minutes, until golden.

6. Brush chicken with more oil mixture, turn and brush other side. Turn potatoes, sprinkle with remaining salt and pepper. Broil 7 to 9 minutes longer, until chicken is no longer pink in the center, juices run clear when thighs are pierced and potatoes are golden and fork-tender.

7. Remove chicken and potatoes to a large heated platter. Arrange carrot and celery sticks on platter or on a separate plate. Pour dressing into a bowl and serve with chicken, potatoes and vegetable sticks.

Makes 4 servings. Per serving: 910 calories, 57 grams protein, 29 grams carbohydrate, 63 grams fat, 177 milligrams cholesterol, 1,018 milligrams sodium

107

Grilled Turkey

Grilling gives turkey a terrific outdoor flavor, even if it's broiled indoors.

⏱ **MAKE-AHEAD**
♥ **LOW-CALORIE**

Grilled Curry-Yogurt Turkey

The high heat of grilling or broiling quickly seals in the turkey juices and keeps the meat moist and tender. The key is not to overcook. Turkey tenderloins are ideal for grilling because they are small enough to cook through quickly yet stay juicy. Each tenderloin has a tough white tendon running down its length. This should be removed with a sharp knife before cooking. Serve Grilled Curry-Yogurt Turkey with rice and a cucumber-and-radish salad.

- 1 cup plain low-fat yogurt
- ¼ cup chicken broth
- 2 tablespoons olive oil
- 2 teaspoons curry powder
- ½ teaspoon salt
- ½ teaspoon pepper
- 2 turkey tenderloins (8 to 10 ounces each), white tendons removed
- 2 teaspoons cornstarch

1. Mix yogurt, broth, oil, curry powder, salt and pepper in a shallow baking dish until blended. Add turkey, turn to coat, then cover and refrigerate at least 3 hours or overnight, turning meat three or four times.

2. Prepare barbecue grill or turn on broiler.

3. Lift turkey from marinade; reserve marinade.

4. To grill: Arrange tenderloins directly on rack 5 to 6 inches from hot coals. Grill 9 to 10 minutes, until lightly browned. Turn and grill 5 to 6 minutes longer, until turkey is browned and no longer pink in the center.

To broil: Put turkey on broiler-pan rack 5 to 6 inches from heat source and broil 9 to 10 minutes. Turn and broil 5 to 6 minutes longer, until turkey is lightly browned and no longer pink in the center.

5. Remove tenderloins to a cutting board and slice against the grain.

6. Meanwhile, pour reserved marinade into a small saucepan, add cornstarch and bring to a boil over medium heat, stirring or whisking constantly. Boil 2 minutes. Pour into a gravy boat and serve separately to spoon over each serving.

Makes 4 servings. Per serving: 251 calories, 33 grams protein, 6 grams carbohydrate, 10 grams fat, 82 milligrams cholesterol, 461 milligrams sodium

Grilled Curry-Yogurt Turkey

Grilled Marinated Turkey Breast

To butterfly turkey breasts, place each half flat on a cutting board, skinned-side down. Holding a long, thin knife parallel to cutting board, slice meat almost all the way through. Open up turkey-breast halves like a book and flatten lightly with the smooth side of a meat mallet. You can serve this dish with a wild-rice casserole flavored with bouillon, chopped celery and onions.

- 1 cup Sauternes wine or apple juice
- ½ cup peanut or vegetable oil
- ½ cup soy sauce
- 1 teaspoon minced fresh garlic
- 1 teaspoon grated fresh gingerroot or 1½ teaspoons ground ginger
- 2 boned and skinned turkey-breast halves (about 1½ pounds each), thawed if frozen, butterflied and flattened to ½- to 1-inch thickness

1. Mix wine, oil, soy sauce, garlic and gingerroot in a large bowl or a doubled plastic food bag. Add turkey and cover bowl or close bag. Marinate at least 1 hour at room temperature or up to 1 day in refrigerator, turning several times.

2. Prepare barbecue grill or turn on broiler.

3. Remove turkey; discard marinade.

4. To grill: Place turkey directly on rack 4 to 6 inches above medium-hot coals. Cover and cook—3 to 5 minutes per side for ½-inch thickness, 5 to 7 minutes per side for 1-inch thickness—until turkey breasts are no longer pink in the center. Take care not to overcook.

To broil: Arrange turkey on broiler-pan rack. Broil 4 to 6 inches from heat source 3 to 5 minutes per side, until turkey breasts are no longer pink in the center.

5. Carve turkey against the grain into long, thin slices and serve.

Makes 6 to 8 servings. Per serving (one-eighth): 331 calories, 56 grams protein, 0 grams carbohydrate, 10 grams fat, 131 milligrams cholesterol, 304 milligrams sodium

Savory Turkey Breast

Serve with slices of crusty bread that have been brushed with olive oil, grilled until toasty and rubbed with a cut clove of garlic. To complete the meal, add your favorite potato salad and juicy sliced tomatoes.

- 1 boned turkey breast with skin (about 4 pounds), thawed if frozen
- 1 teaspoon garlic powder
- 1 teaspoon ground cardamom
- ½ teaspoon ground cumin
- ½ teaspoon ground coriander seed
- ½ teaspoon ground cinnamon
- ½ teaspoon ground ginger
- ¼ teaspoon ground bay leaf
- ¼ teaspoon ground allspice
- ⅛ teaspoon ground cloves

1. Wipe turkey breast dry with paper towels.

2. Mix remaining ingredients in a small bowl. Rub turkey breast with spice mixture. Cover and refrigerate 12 to 24 hours.

3. Prepare barbecue grill or heat oven to 375°F.

4. To prepare grill: Soak 2 cups hickory chips in water for 1 hour. Set a disposable foil drip pan in bottom of barbecue. Arrange about 20 briquettes around each long side of drip pan. Light coals. When coals are hot, add 6 fresh briquettes to each side. Drain hickory chips and scatter over coals.

5. To grill: Place turkey breast skin-side down on rack above drip pan, about 4 to 6 inches above coals. Cover grill and cook 2 to 2½ hours, turning once, until a meat thermometer inserted in thickest part registers 160° to 165°F.

To roast: Place turkey breast skin-side up on rack in a shallow roasting pan. Roast 1 hour. Reduce oven temperature to 325°F. Continue roasting 45 minutes to 1 hour, until a meat thermometer inserted in thickest part registers 160° to 165°F.

6. Transfer to a cutting board. Let turkey stand 15 minutes. Carve thinly. Arrange slices on a heated platter and serve.

Makes 12 servings. Per serving: 225 calories, 33 grams protein, 0 grams carbohydrate, 9 grams fat, 87 milligrams cholesterol, 72 milligrams sodium

Lemon-Thyme Turkey Breast

Serve with grilled corn (see directions). If using dried herbs, mix with 2 teaspoons oil to help spread them evenly under the skin.

1 **whole turkey breast with skin (about 5 pounds), thawed if frozen**
8 **sprigs *each* fresh thyme and Italian flat-leaf parsley (about 2 inches long) or 1 teaspoon *each* dried**
4 **thin slices lemon, halved**

1. Prepare barbecue grill or heat oven to 350°F.

2. Gently run a finger under turkey skin to separate from flesh, leaving skin connected at breastbone. Put 4 sprigs each thyme and parsley and 4 pieces of lemon under turkey skin on each side of breast. Skewer skin to meat along cut edges to prevent shrinkage.

3. To prepare grill: Set an 11⅝x9¼-inch disposable foil drip pan in bottom of barbecue grill. Arrange about 22 briquettes on each long side of drip pan. Set grill 4 to 6 inches above briquettes. Light coals.

4. To grill: Place turkey breast skin-side up directly on rack over drip pan. Cover and cook 2 to 2¼ hours, until a meat thermometer inserted in thickest part, but not touching bone, registers 170°F.

To roast: Place turkey breast skin-side up on a rack in a shallow roasting pan. Roast 1¾ to 2 hours, until a meat thermometer inserted in thickest part, but not touching bone, registers 170°F.

5. Transfer turkey to a cutting board. Let stand 15 minutes. Carve thinly. Arrange slices on a heated platter and serve.

Makes 6 servings with leftovers. Per 4-ounce serving: 225 calories, 33 grams protein, 0 grams carbohydrate, 9 grams fat, 87 milligrams cholesterol, 72 milligrams sodium

Grilled Corn

Pull back husk and remove silk. Smooth husk back in place. If you have time, soak ears in cold water about 30 minutes and drain well. Grill or broil 4 to 6 inches from heat source 15 to 20 minutes, turning three or four times, until the husks are charred and kernels are tender when pierced. Wear gloves or use a towel to peel off the hot husks. If not eating immediately, spread with butter, then wrap in foil and place in a warm oven or on the grill to keep hot.

Lemon-Thyme Turkey Breast

Barbecued Turkey

♥ LOW-CALORIE
✳ MICROWAVE

Barbecued Turkey

Have your butcher saw the turkey in half. Partially cooking the turkey in the oven (or, even better, in the microwave) speeds up the grilling considerably.

1 turkey (12 to 14 pounds), halved
    lengthwise, thawed if frozen
1 teaspoon salt
½ teaspoon pepper
1 envelope (0.7 ounces) Italian salad-
    dressing mix, prepared according
    to package directions
½ cup Sauternes wine, chicken broth
    or water

1. Adjust oven rack to lowest position. Heat oven to 325°F. Have ready a large roasting pan.

2. Arrange turkey halves in roasting pan. Season with salt and pepper. Brush with ¼ cup of the prepared salad dressing; reserve remaining dressing. Pour wine over turkey.

3. Roast 1 to 1½ hours, basting turkey once, until a meat thermometer inserted in thickest part, but not touching bone, registers 135°F. Remove from oven.

4. Meanwhile, prepare grill: Set an 11⅝x9¼-inch disposable foil drip pan in bottom of barbecue. Arrange 22 briquettes on each long side of drip pan. Light coals.

5. To grill: When coals are completely covered with gray ash, pour ½ inch water into drip pan. Arrange turkey halves, skin-side up, over drip pan, directly on rack 4 to 6 inches above hot coals. Cover and grill 1½ to 2 hours, basting with remaining salad dressing four times, until juices run clear when thigh is pierced and a meat thermometer inserted in thickest part of breast, but not touching bone, registers 170°F.

6. Remove to a cutting board. Let stand 30 minutes. Carve and serve.

Makes 12 servings. Per 4-ounce serving (with wine): 298 calories, 30 grams protein, 0 grams carbohydrate, 17 grams fat, 85 milligrams cholesterol, 218 milligrams sodium

Microwave Method: You can partially cook the turkey in the microwave. Sprinkle both sides of one turkey half with some of the salt and pepper. Brush with 2 tablespoons of the salad dressing. Place skin-side up in a 12x8-inch microwave-safe baking dish. Pour ¼ cup of the wine over turkey. Cover loosely with waxed paper. Microwave on high 7 to 10 minutes. Baste with drippings and rotate dish ½ turn. Reduce power to medium-high. Cover and microwave 15 to 18 minutes, rotating dish ½ turn once, until a meat thermometer inserted in thickest part of breast, but not touching bone, registers 135°F. Remove from oven and let stand covered while microwaving second turkey half. Follow grilling directions above.

Turkey Roasted on a Covered Charcoal Grill

On the grill, turkey takes on a distinct smoky flavor. You can cook the turkey stuffed or not. To calculate time, allow about 30 minutes for the fire to be ready, then 13 to 15 minutes cooking time per pound for a stuffed, 14- to 16-pound turkey, about 11 minutes per pound for un-stuffed. Wind direction, temperature and humidity may affect cooking time. For a gas or an electric grill, follow manufacturer's directions for indirect method of cooking. Allow ½ to ¾ pound per person for birds 12 pounds or over, ¾ to 1 pound per person for birds under 12 pounds. The ratio of meat to bone is greater on larger birds. Choose the right-size bird for your grill: There should be at least 1 inch between the turkey and the lid on top and all sides.

1. For a rich, smoky flavor, soak about 2 cups mesquite chips in water for about 1 hour. Put an 11⅝x9¼-inch disposable foil drip pan in bottom of grill. Build a fire of about 30 briquettes (not self-starting) on each long side of drip pan. With vents open and grill uncovered, light coals and let them burn about 30 minutes. The fire is ready when coals are covered with gray ash. Drain chips well and scatter them over the coals.

2. Remove neck and giblets packet from turkey. Rinse, then dry turkey inside and out with paper towels. If roasting it stuffed, loosely spoon stuffing into neck and body cavities. Fold neck skin under back and secure with skewers. Close body cavity with turkey lacers to seal. Tuck wing tips under back; tie legs together with white string. Rub skin all over with oil or unsalted butter or margarine and season with salt and pepper.

3. Place turkey breast-side up on grill and center it over drip pan. Cover grill and cook, adding 9 briquettes to each long side of drip pan every hour, until a meat thermometer inserted in thickest part of thigh, but not touching bone, registers 180° to 185°F and temperature in center of cavity is 160° to 165°F. Remove turkey to a cutting board. Let stand 30 minutes. Carve and serve.

Per 4-ounce serving meat: 298 calories, 30 grams protein, 0 grams carbohydrate, 17 grams fat, 85 milligrams cholesterol, 213 milligrams sodium

Breast of Turkey Teriyaki with Vegetables and Crisp Egg-roll Wrappers

Breast of Turkey Teriyaki with Vegetables and Crisp Egg-roll Wrappers

The teriyaki marinade ensures a crusty exterior and a tender, juicy interior. If cooking on a no-control grill, omit the honey and add ¼ cup oil to the marinade.

- ½ cup soy sauce or tamari
- ½ cup dry sherry
- 2 tablespoons honey
- 1½ tablespoons minced fresh garlic
- 1½ tablespoons minced peeled gingerroot or 1 teaspoon ground ginger
- 1 turkey-breast half (about 2 ½ pounds), skinned, thawed if frozen
- 1½ tablespoons vegetable oil
- 2 medium-size red bell peppers (about 6 ounces each)
- 2 medium-size green bell peppers (about 6 ounces each)
- 4 small zucchini (about 1 pound), halved lengthwise
- 8 egg-roll wrappers
- 16 medium-size green onions

1. Mix soy sauce, sherry, honey, garlic and gingerroot in a medium-size bowl until well blended. Add turkey, skinned-side down. Cover and refrigerate 8 to 24 hours, turning three or four times.

2. Prepare barbecue grill or put oven selector on broil and temperature control at 450°F.

3. Drain turkey; reserve marinade. Brush turkey with oil.

4. To grill: Place turkey bone-side up directly on lightly oiled rack about 5 inches above medium-hot coals. Grill about 15 minutes, until well browned but not charred. Turn, brush with oil, then with some of the reserved marinade. Grill 20 minutes longer.

5. Brush peppers, zucchini and egg-roll wrappers with oil. Arrange bell peppers and zucchini on grill. Grill 10 to 15 minutes, turning zucchini once and peppers three times, until peppers are charred on all sides, zucchini is tender and turkey is well browned (underside may char). Turkey is done when juices run clear when thigh is pierced and a meat thermometer inserted in thickest part, but not touching bone, registers 165° to 170°F. Remove turkey and vegetables to a cutting board, cover with foil. Let stand 10 minutes.

6. Put green onions on grill and grill 5 minutes. Turn onions; add egg-roll wrappers to grill. Grill about 5 minutes, turning egg-roll wrappers once, until onions are browned and crisp-tender and wrappers are crisp with brown spots.

To broil: Place turkey bone-side up on lightly oiled broiler-pan rack. Broil 15 minutes, until well browned. Turn, brush with oil, then with reserved marinade. Broil 20 minutes. Brush peppers, zucchini and egg-roll wrappers with oil. Arrange zucchini and peppers on rack. Broil as described above. Remove turkey and vegetables to a cutting board; cover with foil to keep warm. Broil green onions and egg-roll wrappers as described above.

7. Bring reserved marinade to a boil in a small saucepan. Arrange egg-roll wrappers around edge of a heated platter. Cut bell peppers in quarters and discard seeds. Carve turkey in ¼-inch slices. Arrange turkey, peppers, zucchini and green onions on platter. Pour heated marinade into a small bowl to use as dipping sauce and serve.

Makes 8 servings. Per serving with 2 tablespoons sauce (without wrappers): 261 calories, 35 grams protein, 14 grams carbohydrate, 7 grams fat, 76 milligrams cholesterol, 1,416 milligrams sodium

Potato-Onion Packets

These neat bundles are easy accompaniments to any basic grilled poultry. Make one packet for each serving.

1. For each serving, arrange 1 thinly sliced potato and 1 thinly sliced small onion in layers in the center of an oiled 12-inch-square sheet of foil. Dot with 1 tablespoon butter or margarine and season with ⅛ each teaspoon salt and pepper.

2. Bring up two sides of foil and fold over a few times to seal. Fold over open ends to seal, making a flat packet.

3. Place over medium-hot coals and grill 30 minutes, or until vegetables are tender and browned, turning packet after 15 minutes.

Per serving: 261 calories, 5 grams protein, 36 grams carbohydrate, 12 grams fat, 36 milligrams cholesterol with butter, 0 milligrams cholesterol with margarine, 427 milligrams sodium

Grilled Cornish Hens

⏱ MAKE-AHEAD

Grilled Cornish Hens with Fresh Corn Relish

The corn relish can be made ahead and refrigerated up to three weeks.

Corn Relish

- 3 cups raw corn kernels, cut from 6 medium-size ears
- 1 **each** medium-size red and green bell pepper, finely chopped
- 2 medium-size stalks celery, finely chopped
- 2 jalapeño peppers, seeded and finely chopped (2 tablespoons)
- ⅔ cup cider vinegar
- 3 tablespoons water
- 3 tablespoons granulated sugar
- 1 teaspoon salt
- 1 teaspoon **each** chili powder and ground cumin
- ¼ teaspoon ground cinnamon

Hens

- 3 Cornish hens (about 1½ pounds each), thawed if frozen
- 1 large lime, cut in half
- ¾ teaspoon **each** salt and pepper
- ¾ teaspoon chili powder
- For garnish: lime wedges, jalapeño peppers

1. To make corn relish: Put all ingredients in a medium-size saucepan. Bring to a boil over medium-high heat. Reduce heat to low, cover and simmer 7 to 9 minutes, stirring twice, until vegetables are crisp-tender. Remove from heat and let cool. Refrigerate in a clean jar with a tight-fitting lid or use right away.

2. To make hens: Spoon ¾ cup relish into cavity of each. Tie legs together with white string and tuck wing tips under back. Squeeze juice from lime over hens, then season with salt, pepper and chili powder.

3. Prepare barbecue grill or turn on broiler.

4. To prepare barbecue: Fit a disposable drip pan in bottom of barbecue. Surround with coals and light coals.

5. To grill: Place hens breast-side up over the drip pan on rack 4 to 6 inches above hot coals. Cover grill. Grill hens 55 to 65 minutes, rearranging hens once, until juices run clear when thigh is pierced and a meat thermometer inserted in thickest part, but not touching bone, registers 165° to 170°F.

To broil: Arrange hens on broiler-pan rack. Broil 5 to 6 inches from heat source about 50 minutes, turning and rearranging hens four times, until they test done, as described above. Let stand 10 minutes.

6. To serve: Cut strings and remove. Split hens in half and arrange on plates with the corn relish. Garnish plates with lime wedges and jalapeño peppers.

Makes 6 servings. Per serving with ⅓ cup corn relish: 315 calories, 32 grams protein, 13 grams carbohydrate, 15 grams fat, 123 milligrams cholesterol, 419 milligrams sodium

Grilled Cornish Hens with Fresh Corn Relish

Citrus-Stuffed Cornish Hens with Grilled Green Onions

Cut up some extra citrus fruit for a fresh garnish.

- 1 bottle (16 ounces) Italian salad dressing (2 cups)
- ¼ cup soy sauce
- 4 Cornish hens (1 to 1¼ pounds each), thawed if frozen
- 1½ to 2 cups mesquite chips, soaked in water 1 to 2 hours (optional)
- 1 small orange, cut in 1-inch chunks
- 1 lime, cut in 1-inch chunks
- 1 medium-size lemon, cut in 1-inch chunks

Grilled Green Onions (recipe follows)

1. Mix dressing and soy sauce in a large bowl. Add hens, cover and marinate about 2 hours in refrigerator, turning twice.

2. Prepare barbecue grill or turn on broiler.

3. To prepare grill: Set an 11⅝x9¼-inch disposable foil drip pan in the center of the bottom of barbecue grill to catch drippings. Arrange about 15 briquettes on each long side of drip pan. Light briquettes. When coals are completely covered with gray ash (about 30 minutes), pour ½ inch water into drip pan. Drain mesquite chips, if using, and scatter over coals. Set grill rack 4 to 6 inches above coals.

4. Remove hens and reserve marinade.

5. Stuff body cavities with citrus chunks. Tie legs together with white string and tuck wing tips under back.

6. To grill: Arrange hens breast-side up on rack over drip pan. Cover and grill 60 to 70 minutes, rearranging hens and basting with reserved marinade four times, until juices run clear when thigh is pierced and a meat thermometer inserted in thickest part, but not touching bone, registers 165° to 170°F.

To broil: Arrange hens breast-side up on broiler-pan rack. Broil 4 to 5 inches from heat source 50 to 60 minutes, rearranging hens and basting four times, until juices run clear when thigh is pierced.

7. Cut strings, remove fruit from cavities and leave hens whole or split in half. Arrange on a heated platter. Serve with Grilled Green Onions.

Makes 4 servings. Per serving: 494 calories, 48 grams protein, 3 grams carbohydrate, 31 grams fat, 175 milligrams cholesterol, 1,395 milligrams sodium

Grilled Green Onions

- ¾ cup bottled Italian dressing
- 2 tablespoons soy sauce
- 2 tablespoons lemon juice
- 12 large green onions, trimmed

1. Mix dressing, soy sauce and lemon juice in a long shallow dish. Add green onions and turn to coat. Marinate 15 to 20 minutes.

2. Prepare barbecue grill or turn on broiler.

3. Remove onions; reserve marinade.

4. To grill: Grill onions directly on rack about 5 inches above medium-hot coals 10 to 12 minutes, turning and basting four times, until tender and slightly charred.

To broil: Arrange on broiler-pan rack and broil 4 to 5 inches from heat source 10 to 12 minutes, turning and basting four times, until tender and slightly charred.

5. Arrange on platter around hens.

Makes 4 servings. Per serving: 80 calories, 1 gram protein, 8 grams carbohydrate, 5 grams fat, 0 milligrams cholesterol, 301 milligrams sodium

Citrus-Stuffed Cornish Hens with Grilled Green Onions

In the Microwave

More than 70 percent of homes have at least one microwave oven, but most are used only to heat water, make popcorn and bake potatoes. Your microwave can do so much more: It can cook all or part of your dinner, cut down on cleanup time and improve the taste and nutritional value of your foods.

Herbed Crumbed Chicken

Microwaving Tips

☐ **Wattage:** Our recipes were tested in a 650-watt oven. If yours has a lower wattage, you'll need to increase the cooking time. In a 500-watt oven, increase time by 20 to 30 percent; a 400-watt oven, increase time by about 40 percent. Start checking food for doneness at the minimum time range given in recipe.

☐ **Cookware:** Best shapes are round or oval, not oblong or square, though those can be used. Be sure to use microwave-safe cookware. Don't microwave in metal (unless your oven is specifically made for metal) or in flimsy, flexible plastic take-out containers.

☐ **Covering:** When covering food, follow recipe suggestions. Use only plastic wraps specifically made for the microwave, and never let them touch the food. Turn back one corner to vent. When uncovering food, remove cover from the side of dish farthest away from you and avert your face to avoid a steam burn.

☐ **Rotating:** If your oven has a turntable, this step will not be necessary; otherwise, follow recipe instructions and rotate the dish in the same direction each time.

☐ **Arranging and Rearranging:** Correct arrangement and rearrangement of food is necessary to allow the food to cook evenly, especially important for large pieces of poultry. Follow recipe instructions.

☐ **Standing Time:** This is an important step because more heat is retained in food in microwave cooking than in conventional cooking. Poultry should be removed from the microwave a few minutes before it is done, while it is still slightly pink in the center or near the bone. While the food stands, the temperature will be equalized throughout the dish and the heat from the outer layers will penetrate to the center. A word of caution: It is not healthy to eat undercooked poultry. If there is still some pink in the center after the standing time, return the dish to the microwave for further cooking. However, very young chickens will retain some red around the bones even when cooked through.

Quick Cutlets

Speed your way through dinner preparation with these two time-savers: ready-to-cook boneless chicken breasts and the microwave oven.

♥ **LOW-CALORIE**
✳ **MICROWAVE**

Herbed Crumbed Chicken

¼ cup grated Parmesan or
    Romano cheese
¼ cup wheat germ (see Note)
1 tablespoon chopped fresh parsley
1 teaspoon dried oregano leaves,
    crumbled
¼ teaspoon garlic powder
2 tablespoons margarine
4 boned and skinned chicken-breast
    halves (about 1¼ pounds)
For garnish: lemon wedges, fresh
    parsley sprigs

1. Mix cheese, wheat germ, parsley, oregano and garlic powder in a small bowl.

2. Melt margarine on high in a small microwave-safe cup or bowl.

3. Brush both sides of chicken with melted margarine, then dip in cheese mixture to coat. Arrange spoke-fashion in an 8-inch square microwave-safe baking dish, with thicker parts toward outer edge. Sprinkle any remaining crumb mixture over top. Cover with a paper towel.

4. Microwave on high 6 to 7 minutes, rotating dish ½ turn after 5 minutes, until chicken is barely opaque and slightly pink in the center of the thickest part when tested with a knife. Let stand 3 minutes or until chicken is opaque and loses its pink color. Arrange on a heated platter, garnish with lemon wedges and parsley sprigs.

Makes 4 servings. Per serving: 259 calories, 37 grams protein, 4 grams carbohydrate, 10 grams fat, 86 milligrams cholesterol, 253 milligrams sodium

Note: Packaged plain bread crumbs can be used instead of the wheat germ.

Vegetable-Stuffed Chicken Breasts

½ cup finely chopped onion
½ cup finely chopped celery
½ cup finely chopped carrot
1 tablespoon butter or margarine
¼ cup light cream cheese, at room temperature
2 tablespoons grated Parmesan cheese
2 tablespoons chopped fresh parsley
½ teaspoon grated fresh lemon peel
⅛ teaspoon salt
⅛ teaspoon pepper
4 boned and skinned chicken-breast halves (about 4 ounces each)
¾ cup chicken broth
1 tablespoon lemon juice
½ teaspoon cornstarch

1. Put onion, celery, carrot and butter in a 9-inch microwave-safe pie plate. Cover with waxed paper. Microwave on high 4 to 5 minutes, stirring twice, until vegetables are tender.

2. Mix cream cheese, Parmesan, parsley, lemon peel, salt and pepper in a medium-size bowl until blended. Add vegetables.

3. Cut each breast half horizontally to within ¼ inch of opposite side to make a pocket. Spread about ¼ cup of the filling in each pocket. Secure with toothpicks.

4. Arrange spoke-fashion in same pie plate. Pour ½ cup of the broth and the lemon juice over chicken. Cover with waxed paper.

5. Microwave on high 5 to 7 minutes, rotating plate ¼ turn three times, until chicken is firm. Remove chicken to a heated platter and keep warm.

6. Mix cornstarch and remaining ¼ cup broth until smooth. Stir into juices in pie plate. Microwave on high 3 to 5 minutes, stirring every minute, until thickened. Spoon sauce over chicken and serve.

Makes 4 servings. Per serving with 3 tablespoons sauce: 286 calories, 40 grams protein, 5 grams carbohydrate, 11 grams fat, 117 milligrams cholesterol with butter, 108 milligrams cholesterol with margarine, 393 milligrams sodium

Divine Chicken

Divine Chicken

½ cup packaged Italian-style dry bread crumbs
⅓ cup grated Parmesan cheese
2 tablespoons chopped fresh parsley
⅛ teaspoon pepper
⅛ teaspoon garlic powder
¼ cup butter or margarine
3 tablespoons lemon juice
1 pound thin-sliced chicken-breast cutlets

1. Mix crumbs, cheese, parsley, pepper and garlic powder on a sheet of waxed paper.

2. Melt butter on high in a microwave-safe pie plate. Stir in lemon juice.

3. Dip cutlets in butter mixture, then coat in crumb mixture. Roll up each cutlet, starting from a narrow end.

4. Line a 10-inch round microwave-safe plate with a double layer of paper towels. Arrange chicken rolls seam-side down in spoke-fashion on lined plate. Cover loosely with waxed paper.

5. Microwave on medium-high 5 to 7 minutes, rotating plate ¼ turn twice, until chicken is firm and barely opaque when tested with a knife. Uncover and let stand 5 minutes, until no longer pink in the center.

Makes 4 servings. Per serving: 375 calories, 40 grams protein, 11 grams carbohydrate, 18 grams fat, 133 milligrams cholesterol with butter, 99 milligrams cholesterol with margarine, 366 milligrams sodium

International Microwaving

※ **MICROWAVE**
Chicken Breasts Parmesan

To accompany the chicken, tear a large head of escarole into bite-size pieces, wash well and cook in olive oil with minced fresh garlic in a large skillet over high heat until wilted, or cook in a shallow dish in the microwave.

- 1 **can (8 ounces) tomato sauce**
- 1 **teaspoon Italian dried-herb seasoning**
- ¼ **teaspoon garlic powder**
- ½ **cup cornflake crumbs**
- ¼ **cup grated Parmesan cheese**
- 1 **teaspoon dried parsley flakes**
- 4 **chicken-breast halves (about 10 ounces each), skinned**
- 1 **large egg, lightly beaten**
- ½ **cup shredded mozzarella cheese (2 ounces)**

1. Mix tomato sauce, Italian seasoning and garlic powder in a 2-cup microwave-safe measure or bowl.

2. Cover loosely with waxed paper and microwave on high 2 minutes. Stir; reduce power to medium and microwave 4 to 5 minutes, stirring once, until simmering.

3. Mix cornflake crumbs, Parmesan and parsley on a sheet of waxed paper. Dip chicken in egg, then coat in crumb mixture.

4. Arrange pieces meaty-side up in a single layer in an 11x7-inch microwave-safe baking dish, with thicker parts toward outer edge.

5. Cover loosely with waxed paper and microwave on medium-high 5 minutes.

6. Rearrange pieces (do not turn over), bringing those in the center to the outer edge.

7. Cover loosely. Rotate dish ½ turn and microwave on medium-high 4 to 9 minutes longer, until meat is opaque but still slightly pink near the bone.

8. Pour sauce over chicken and sprinkle with mozzarella. Microwave uncovered on high 2 to 4 minutes, until mozzarella melts and chicken is no longer pink in the center.

Makes 4 servings. Per serving: 482 calories, 62 grams protein, 16 grams carbohydrate, 17 grams fat, 213 milligrams cholesterol, 715 milligrams sodium

Chicken Breasts Parmesan

✳ MICROWAVE
Chicken Cacciatore

Serve over pasta or rice.

---

1 medium-size green bell pepper,
    thinly sliced (about 1 cup)
1 medium-size onion, thinly sliced
    (about ¾ cup)
1 tablespoon olive oil
2 tablespoons all-purpose flour
1 can (28 ounces) tomatoes
½ cup dry red wine or water
1 tablespoon dried parsley flakes
1 teaspoon minced fresh garlic
1 teaspoon paprika
½ teaspoon salt
½ teaspoon dried oregano leaves
¼ teaspoon pepper
¼ teaspoon dried basil leaves
2 whole chicken breasts (about 2½
    pounds), skin and visible fat
    removed, each cut in 4 pieces

1. Put bell pepper, onion and oil in a shallow 3-quart microwave-safe baking dish. Cover with a lid or vented plastic wrap.

2. Microwave on high 3 to 4 minutes, stirring once, until vegetables are crisp-tender.

3. Stir in flour until blended, then remaining ingredients except chicken.

4. Cover and microwave on high 4 to 5 minutes, stirring once, until mixture comes to a boil.

5. Arrange chicken on top in a single layer, with thickest parts toward outer edge of dish. Cover with a lid or vented plastic wrap.

6. Microwave on high 5 to 6 minutes. Turn chicken over and rearrange, bringing center pieces to outer edge. Spoon sauce from bottom over chicken.

7. Cover and microwave 5 to 6 minutes longer. (Chicken should be opaque but still slightly pink near the bone.) Let stand covered 5 minutes, until chicken is no longer pink, and serve.

Makes 4 servings. Per serving: 306 calories, 40 grams protein, 14 grams carbohydrate, 7 grams fat, 129 milligrams cholesterol, 530 milligrams sodium

🕐 MAKE-AHEAD
✳ MICROWAVE
Santa Fe Chicken

The bean mixture can be prepared and refrigerated up to two days ahead.

---

1 cup dried black beans, picked over
    and rinsed
Water
2 tablespoons fresh-squeezed
    lime juice
1 tablespoon olive oil
1 tablespoon chopped fresh parsley
1 tablespoon chopped fresh cilantro or
    additional parsley
1 teaspoon minced fresh garlic
1 teaspoon dried oregano leaves
½ teaspoon chili powder
½ teaspoon ground cumin
4 boned and skinned chicken-breast
    halves (about 4 ounces each)
1 lemon, thinly sliced

1. Put beans in a deep 4-quart microwave-safe casserole or bowl. Add water to cover. Cover with a lid or vented plastic wrap.

2. Microwave on high 8 to 10 minutes, until water is boiling. Boil 3 minutes. Let stand covered 1 hour and drain.

3. Add 4 cups fresh water to beans. Cover and microwave on high 10 to 12 minutes, until water has come to a full boil. Let stand 1 minute, then carefully stir with a long-handled spoon.

4. Reduce power to medium. Cover and microwave 1 hour and 20 minutes to 1 hour and 30 minutes, stirring three times, until beans are tender. Let stand 5 minutes. Drain and stir in remaining ingredients except chicken and lemon. (The bean mixture can be refrigerated at this point.)

5. Arrange chicken spoke-fashion in a 9-inch microwave-safe pie plate, with thicker portions toward outer edge. Place a lemon slice on each. Cover with a lid or vented plastic wrap.

6. Microwave on high 5 to 7 minutes, rotating plate ¼ turn three times, until chicken is almost opaque in the thickest part. Let stand 5 minutes, until no longer pink in the center. Discard lemon.

7. Put chicken on a cutting board and slice in strips. Arrange chicken on top of the bean mixture and serve.

Makes 4 servings. Per serving: 366 calories, 42 grams protein, 31 grams carbohydrate, 7 grams fat, 90 milligrams cholesterol, 76 milligrams sodium

Chicken Quesadillas

If avocados are firm, let them ripen at room temperature. It may take two to four days before they yield to gentle pressure; then they should be kept in the refrigerator.

---

    6 tablespoons fresh-squeezed
        lime juice
    2 tablespoons finely chopped onion
    1 teaspoon ground cumin
    1 teaspoon chili powder
 1¼ pounds boned and skinned
        chicken-breast halves, cut in
        narrow strips
    2 small avocados (or 1 large), halved,
        pitted, peeled and cut in ½-inch
        pieces
    1 pound fresh tomatoes, chopped
  ¼ cup chopped fresh cilantro
Four 6- to 8-inch flour tortillas
  ¾ cup shredded Monterey Jack
        cheese
Sour cream (optional)

1. Mix 4 tablespoons of the lime juice, the onion, cumin and chili powder in a 2-quart microwave-safe bowl. Stir in chicken, let marinate 15 minutes.

2. Meanwhile, mix avocados, tomatoes, cilantro and remaining 2 tablespoons lime juice in a medium-size bowl.

3. Cover chicken with a lid or vented plastic wrap. Microwave on high 4 to 6 minutes, stirring once, until chicken is no longer pink in the center.

4. Stack tortillas between paper towels and microwave on high 1 to 1½ minutes, until hot.

5. Put each tortilla on a microwave-safe plate. Sprinkle each with ¼ of the cheese. Microwave each about 30 seconds, just until the cheese starts to melt.

6. Spoon some of the chicken mixture over each tortilla, top with some of the tomato mixture and sour cream, if desired, and serve.

Makes 4 servings. Per serving (without sour cream): 528 calories, 54 grams protein, 28 grams carbohydrate, 26 grams fat, 132 milligrams cholesterol, 219 milligrams sodium

Chicken Quesadillas

Oriental Stir-fry

Serve over brown or white rice or with crisp chow-mein noodles.

2½ **cups 1-inch fresh broccoli florets (5 ounces)**
½ **cup finely sliced green onions**
½ **cup thinly sliced carrot**
½ **cup sliced green bell pepper**
½ **cup sliced mushrooms**
½ **teaspoon grated fresh gingerroot**
½ **teaspoon minced fresh garlic**
1 **pound boned and skinned chicken-breast halves, cut in ¼-inch-wide strips**

Sauce

1 **cup chicken broth**
2 **tablespoons low-sodium soy sauce**
2 **tablespoons cornstarch**
1 **tablespoon dry sherry (optional)**
½ **teaspoon granulated sugar (optional)**

1. Put vegetables, gingerroot and garlic in a deep 2-quart microwave-safe casserole. Cover with a lid or vented plastic wrap.

2. Microwave on high 3 to 4 minutes, stirring once, until vegetables are crisp-tender.

3. Stir in chicken. Cover and microwave on high 2 to 3 minutes, stirring once, until outside of chicken is no longer pink.

4. Meanwhile, mix all sauce ingredients in a small bowl until smooth. Stir into chicken until blended.

5. Cover and microwave 2 to 4 minutes, stirring once, until sauce is thickened and clear. Let stand covered 2 minutes. Transfer to plates and serve.

Makes 4 servings. Per serving (without sherry and sugar): 247 calories, 39 grams protein, 12 grams carbohydrate, 4 grams fat, 93 milligrams cholesterol, 550 milligrams sodium

Singapore Chicken

Serve this mildly spiced curry over rice with small bowls of mango chutney, raisins and almonds as accompaniments.

2 **tablespoons olive or vegetable oil**
4 **teaspoons curry powder**
2 **cups sliced onions**
1 **pound boned and skinned chicken-breast halves, trimmed of visible fat and cut in 3x1-inch strips**
1 **can (8 ounces) pineapple chunks in juice, drained; juice reserved**
1 **tablespoon cornstarch**
1 **cup fresh or canned mung-bean sprouts, rinsed and drained**
2 **tablespoons reduced-sodium soy sauce**

1. Mix oil and 3 teaspoons of the curry powder in a deep 3-quart microwave-safe casserole. Microwave on high 1 minute.

2. Stir in onions. Cover with a lid or vented plastic wrap and microwave on high 6 to 9 minutes, stirring twice, until tender.

3. Stir in chicken. Cover and microwave on high 3 to 4 minutes, stirring once, until chicken is no longer pink.

4. Mix reserved pineapple juice and cornstarch until smooth. Stir into chicken mixture.

5. Cover and microwave on high 1 to 1½ minutes, stirring once, until juices are slightly thickened.

6. Stir in pineapple chunks, bean sprouts, soy sauce and remaining 1 teaspoon curry powder. Cover and microwave 2 minutes, stirring once, until hot. Let stand covered 5 minutes. Serve over rice.

Makes 4 servings. Per serving: 272 calories, 29 grams protein, 20 grams carbohydrate, 9 grams fat, 66 milligrams cholesterol, 379 milligrams sodium

✳ MICROWAVE
Chicken à la Suisse

Serve with buttered broccoli spears or a mixed-green salad.

- ⅓ **cup buttermilk baking mix**
- 1½ **teaspoons paprika**
- ¼ **teaspoon pepper**
- 6 **boned and skinned chicken-breast halves (about 4 ounces each)**
- 3 **thin slices (1 ounce each) fully cooked ham, halved crosswise**
- 3 **thin slices (1 ounce each) Swiss cheese, halved crosswise**
- ½ **cup dry white wine or chicken broth**
- 1 **tablespoon cornstarch**
- 1 **cup half-and-half**
- 1 **tablespoon chopped fresh parsley (optional)**

1. Stir baking mix, paprika and pepper in a shallow bowl or pie plate until blended.

2. Put chicken breasts in a single layer between two sheets of waxed paper. With a meat mallet or the bottom of a heavy saucepan, flatten to ¼-inch thickness.

3. Top each piece of chicken with a half slice each of ham and cheese; trim edges to fit. Roll up chicken from narrow end. Roll in seasoned baking mix to coat.

4. Arrange chicken seam-side down in an 8-inch square microwave-safe baking dish.

5. Cover loosely with waxed paper and microwave on high 8 minutes, rotating dish ½ turn once during cooking.

6. Pour in wine. Cover loosely and microwave 4 to 6 minutes longer, until chicken is firm and barely opaque in the center. Remove chicken to a cutting board. Cover and keep warm.

7. Stir cornstarch into half-and-half until smooth. Gradually blend into liquid in baking dish.

8. Microwave on high 3 to 5 minutes, stirring every minute, until thickened. Stir in parsley, if desired.

9. Spoon sauce onto plates. Slice chicken rolls, arrange over the sauce and serve.

Makes 6 servings. Per serving (with wine): 404 calories, 45 grams protein, 10 grams carbohydrate, 19 grams fat, 133 milligrams cholesterol, 458 milligrams sodium

Chicken à la Suisse

Microwave Instead of Roast

✳ MICROWAVE

Crisp-Coated Chicken Drumsticks

This dish would go well with a shredded cabbage-and-carrot slaw tossed with golden raisins and a pinch of cinnamon, dressed with mayonnaise and red-wine vinegar.

16 round buttery crackers, finely
     crushed (⅔ cup)
1½ tablespoons dry mustard
  1 teaspoon paprika
  1 large egg
  2 tablespoons milk
1½ pounds chicken drumsticks
Mustard Sauce (recipe follows)

1. Mix cracker crumbs, mustard and paprika on a sheet of waxed paper.

2. Beat egg and milk with a fork in a shallow bowl.

3. Dip each drumstick in egg mixture, then coat with crumb mixture.

4. Arrange drumsticks spoke-fashion on a microwave-safe roasting rack with sides, with meatier portions toward outer edge.

5. Microwave on high about 14 minutes (8 to 10 minutes per pound), rotating rack ½ turn once halfway through cooking time. Chicken should be slightly pink near the bone. Let stand uncovered 5 minutes, until no longer pink in the center.

6. Serve with Mustard Sauce on the side.

Makes 4 servings. Per serving with 1½ tablespoons sauce: 342 calories, 34 grams protein, 18 grams carbohydrate, 14 grams fat, 151 milligrams cholesterol, 413 milligrams sodium

Mustard Sauce

3 tablespoons grape jelly
3 tablespoons prepared mustard

1. Put jelly in a 1-cup microwave-safe glass measure. Microwave on high 30 to 40 seconds, until melted.

2. Stir in mustard and microwave 30 seconds to develop flavor. Let sauce stand 1 minute. Stir sauce and serve with the chicken.

Makes about ⅓ cup.

✳ MICROWAVE

Chicken with Dressing

Serve with hot chicken gravy.

3 tablespoons butter or margarine
2 pounds chicken thighs
¼ cup chopped onion
¼ cup finely diced celery
1 package (8 ounces) corn-bread
    stuffing mix
1 large egg
½ teaspoon salt
¼ teaspoon poultry seasoning
¼ teaspoon pepper

1. Melt 1 tablespoon of the butter in a deep 3-quart microwave-safe casserole or bowl.

2. Add chicken thighs and turn to coat in butter.

3. Cover with a lid or vented plastic wrap and microwave on high 12 to 14 minutes, rearranging chicken once, until no longer pink near the bone when tested with the tip of a small knife.

4. Let stand uncovered until cool enough to handle.

5. Pour pan drippings into a 2-cup glass measure. Add water to reach the 1½-cup mark.

6. Pull skin off chicken. Remove meat from bones and tear into strips.

7. Add remaining 2 tablespoons butter, the onion and celery to same casserole. Cover and microwave on high 4 to 5 minutes, stirring twice, until vegetables are tender.

8. Add stuffing mix, egg, salt, poultry seasoning, pepper and the 1½ cups drippings mixture. Stir until well mixed and stuffing is moistened. Cover with a lid or vented plastic wrap and microwave on high 3 to 4 minutes, until hot.

9. Add chicken and toss gently to mix. Cover and microwave on high 2 minutes. Let stand covered 5 minutes before serving.

Makes 6 servings. Per serving: 466 calories, 26 grams protein, 30 grams carbohydrate, 26 grams fat, 151 milligrams cholesterol with butter, 135 milligrams cholesterol with margarine, 773 milligrams sodium

Roast Chicken with Stuffing and Gravy

✳ **MICROWAVE**

Roast Chicken with Stuffing and Gravy

For crisp, browned skin, place cooked chicken in a conventional oven 5 to 10 minutes at 500°F.

> 1 broiler-fryer chicken (about 3½ pounds)
> 1 teaspoon salt
> ½ teaspoon pepper
> Poultry Stuffing (recipe follows)
> 3 tablespoons butter or margarine, melted
> 1 teaspoon paprika
> Chicken Gravy (recipe follows)

1. Remove giblets package from chicken. Dry chicken well inside and out with paper towels. Sprinkle body cavity with half the salt and pepper.

2. Spoon stuffing into cavity. Tuck wing tips under the back and tie the legs together with white string.

3. Mix butter and paprika and brush over chicken. Sprinkle with remaining salt and pepper.

4. Place chicken breast-side down on a microwave-safe roasting rack with sides or in a 12x8x2-inch microwave-safe baking dish.

5. Microwave uncovered on high 10 minutes. Turn chicken breast-side up.

6. Microwave on high 10 to 12 minutes longer, until chicken is tender and drumstick moves easily.

7. Cover chicken loosely with a foil tent. Let stand 10 minutes, until juices run clear when inner thigh is pierced and a meat thermometer inserted in the center of stuffing registers 165°F.

8. Carve chicken and serve with the gravy.

Makes 4 servings. Per serving: 490 calories, 46 grams protein, 13 grams carbohydrate, 28 grams fat, 224 milligrams cholesterol with butter, 161 milligrams cholesterol with margarine, 1,383 milligrams sodium

Poultry Stuffing

> 2 tablespoons butter or margarine
> ⅓ cup chopped onion
> ⅓ cup diced celery
> 2 cups dry bread cubes or crumbled day-old corn bread
> 3 tablespoons finely chopped fresh parsley
> ¼ teaspoon dried sage leaves
> ¼ teaspoon dried thyme leaves
> ¼ teaspoon pepper
> ⅛ teaspoon salt
> ½ cup chicken broth

1. Put butter, onion and celery in a 3-quart microwave-safe casserole. Cover tightly with a lid or vented plastic wrap and microwave on high 3 to 4 minutes, until vegetables are crisp-tender.

2. Stir bread cubes and seasonings into vegetables.

3. Pour broth into a 2-cup glass measure. Microwave on high 2 to 3 minutes, until boiling. Pour over bread mixture and stir well to moisten.

Makes 2 cups of stuffing, enough for a 3½- to 4-pound chicken.

Chicken Gravy

> 2 tablespoons chicken-fat drippings or melted butter or margarine
> 2 tablespoons all-purpose flour
> Defatted pan juices plus enough chicken broth to equal 1 cup
> ½ teaspoon soy sauce
> ¼ teaspoon celery salt
> ⅛ teaspoon pepper

1. Whisk fat drippings and flour in a 1-quart glass measure until smooth. Whisk in remaining ingredients.

2. Microwave on high 5 to 8 minutes, stirring three times, until thickened and bubbly.

Makes 1 cup.

Index

For information on how you can have **Better Homes and Gardens** delivered to your door, write to:
Mr. Robert Austin, P.O. Box 4536, Des Moines, IA 50336